PRAISE FOR *EXTREME WILDERNESS SURVIVAL*

"Craig Caudill's *Extreme Wilderness Survival* is a great intro to all things survival and tactical for the extremes, covering not only the fundamentals of survival but also new subjects traditionally reserved only for the military. It is sure to get everyone thinking about some new aspects of the overall survival situation they may encounter."

—**MYKEL HAWKE,** U.S. Army Special Forces Combat Veteran, Author and Host of *Lost Survivors*

"Craig Caudill knows from hard-won experience what works and what doesn't. If I were in a true survival situation, I can't think of another instructor I'd want by my side."

—**JIM COBB,** Author of *Prepper's Long-Term Survival Guide*

"The quality of information in this book will keep you safe in a 'time is life' scenario. I highly recommend this manual to be read more than once and to be studied regularly."

—**MAJOR RODNEY VAN ZANT,** Special Response Team Leader, Owner of Iron Sight Defense

"It is with great pleasure that I recommend Craig Caudill's book *Extreme Wilderness Survival*. Craig shares a solid knowledge on wilderness survival skills."

—**MIKE HULL,** Law Enforcement Officer, Owner of VITALE LLC and Author of *Man Tracking in Law Enforcement*

EXTREME WILDERNESS SURVIVAL

ESSENTIAL KNOWLEDGE TO SURVIVE ANY OUTDOOR SITUATION
SHORT-TERM OR LONG-TERM, WITH OR WITHOUT GEAR
AND ALONE OR WITH OTHERS

CRAIG CAUDILL

FOUNDER AND CHIEF INSTRUCTOR OF NATURE RELIANCE SCHOOL

PAGE STREET
PUBLISHING CO.

PAGE STREET
PUBLISHING CO.

First published in 2017 by
Page Street Publishing Co.
27 Congress Street, Suite 105
Salem, MA 01970
www.pagestreetpublishing.com

Distributed by Macmillan, sales in Canada by The Canadian Manda Group.

20   19   18   17   3   4

ISBN-13: 978-1-62414-336-6
ISBN-10: 1-62414-336-9

Library of Congress Control Number: 2016950608

Cover and book design by Page Street Publishing Co.
Photography by Aaron Sole and Shutterstock

Printed and bound in China

Page Street is proud to be a member of 1% for the Planet. Members donate one percent of their sales to one or more of the over 1,500 environmental and sustainability charities across the globe who participate in this program.

TO MY WIFE, WHO HAS SUPPORTED
AND ENCOURAGED ME LIKE NO OTHER

CONTENTS

INTRODUCTION

Various studies have proven as irrefutable fact that being in the wilderness is healthy, and not only from a purely physical perspective, either. Many people have found incredible growth in mind, body and spirit by wilderness travel. Challenges and rewards await those who endeavor to spend more time hiking, hunting and otherwise enjoying a rural, wooded environment.

I must also note that there are numerous stories of people perishing, being injured or becoming sick in these same types of environments. My goal for you is to spend more time outside and gain the benefits while avoiding the pitfalls that so many ignore and pay dearly for.

I have spent the better part of four decades outdoors. I am a wilderness scientist of sorts, constantly studying the effects of wilderness experiences on my own mind-set, skills, tactics and gear. I have spent several weeks in the wilderness with nothing more than a knife, "living off the land." Each year, I teach outdoor pursuits to hundreds of people of varying skill and age levels and I have experienced much that needs to be shared.

In this book, you will have the opportunity to gather insight into what it takes to comfortably make it in the outdoors. I will help you strengthen your mind-set first. It is absolutely critical to your survival. Use this book at home or in the woods as a resource to build your skills and ability to work with others. I will also detail the systems of carry for modern and primitive gear that will make your wilderness stay more comfortable.

You will learn from my experiences, and those of others, as I share survival stories from the real world. I will then break each story down and determine what went right and what went wrong. In this manner, you can keep yourself and those you care for out of danger. I will also discuss the many aspects of wilderness survival, including primitive and modern methodology for personal safety, shelter, water and food.

At my Nature Reliance School, our motto has always been, "Where practical meets natural." This book is an extension of that. You will learn what works from old-school primitive means when there is no equipment available alongside more modern methods and gear. My goal is for everyone in the world to be more self-reliant. It brings you power, it brings you comfort and it makes you more prepared.

Another favorite mind-set of my school community is, "Come on, join in, let's learn together." I thank you for joining me in that endeavor. I am most honored and humbled you have chosen this book to help you.

Craig Caudill

SECTION I

MIND-SET DEVELOPMENT

Survival and survival training are two different things altogether. One is real life, the other is preparation for real life. During any survival-related event, stress will be the inevitable companion. What you will need to do in survival training and preparation is develop systems of study so that you can control and minimize the stress as much as possible. These systems of study will assist you in thinking clearly and making appropriate decisions while under stress. Consider your mind a filing cabinet and survival skills a folder in that cabinet. When you experience anything new (such as a survival situation), your mind goes through the folders looking for answers on what to do. If your mind finds something that relates to the situation, it will use information in that folder to direct the mind and body to do something. If it doesn't, it finds the closest resemblance to the experience and acts that out. What you want to do with these systems is prepare your mind before you ever experience an event to break it down and apply information from the correct folder. This will help you as you move forward in the book to develop the right system of study first. Develop and strengthen your mind, then move on to the skills, tactics and gear you need to complete this survival training folder. This will enable you to carry around information wherever you may go.

CHAPTER 1

THE PROVEN SYSTEMS OF SURVIVAL STUDY

KEEP IT SIMPLE, STUPID.
—ANONYMOUS

Alaska can make or break an outdoorsperson in the same amount of time it takes to brush your teeth. Mount Foraker in Alaska rises 17,400 feet (5,303 m) into the air alongside the other wonderful mountain monuments of the Central Range within Denali National Park. It is there that three climbers were making their attempt at a new route to the peak. Shortly before the summit was made, a very strong storm brought in high winds and blinding snow. This was incredibly problematic, since the ice conditions made it such that proper safety equipment could not be attached to the mountain. The three climbers, simply roped to one another, made their way as best they could. A decision was made to abort the summit attempt. However, an avalanche struck and threw them down the mountain.

When one of the climbers awoke, he discovered that one of his best friends was dead and the other friend was presumed so. Upon further searching, the presumption proved true, and this climber now found himself with a fractured foot, nearly 800 feet (244 m) from where the slide had begun.

He immediately gathered himself, found a small shelter, got into one of his teammates' sleeping bags and fell asleep. Upon waking he melted some snow for hydration and cooked some food. All of this took nearly 36 hours to complete. Upon setting out on his descent, the climber discovered many other obstacles and areas nearly impossible to move across or over. However, after six days of incredible mental and physical fortitude, he made his way to safety.

Let's break this down and consider what went right and what went wrong. There is plenty of each to learn from this particular event.

The first lesson we can glean from this experience is understanding how you should go about making decisions in a stressful situation. One of the best methods for making decisions is what many in the military refer to as the Combat Rule of Three. (For our training, I usually refer to this as the Critical Rule of Three since most of our decision making does not occur during combat.)

At its essence, the Critical Rule of Three means if you see three anomalies—three things out of the ordinary—you should make a decision to change things up with no hesitation. In our story above, the climbers realized that one form of security equipment would not work. They tried another and it did not work. They then noticed a storm was coming their way. Those were their three anomalies. It's unknown how much hesitation they felt to turn around. Much applause to the three climbers for making the right decision to turn around at this point and head back down. However, their downfall came in not recognizing an unsafe area near an avalanche-prone zone. What was missed?

It can be assumed that there was a bit of an adrenaline junkie in all of the climbers. Why else would anyone go into subzero temps, high winds and avalanche-laden mountains seeking the next summit? That is why your number one priority in all survival situations should be personal safety.

Let's get into how you can do a better job of taking care of yourself through systems of survival.

SYSTEMS OF SAFETY AND SURVIVAL

A system of any kind is an assemblage or set of correlated pieces. These pieces can be physical components, such as a car engine, or more intangible components, such as the system of traffic laws that you follow. (For example, we all drive on a certain side of the road.) What you need for a proper study on the topic of survival is a system by which you can mentally have the right components and physically have the skills and gear to develop two systems that work together. The reason I like to work on our systems of survival is because, quite frankly, our brains are incredible information processors. While a supercomputer might beat our neural network when it comes to speed, what that same computer does not have is hundreds of linked processors that can equal our brain. This is what neurologists refer to as parallel processing. To explain this more easily, let's consider you reading these words. Your eyes are moving across the sentence, your hands are holding the book (or electronic device), you can hear the things going on around you, you can feel the temperature of your location and so on. We could probably note a minimum of one hundred items that your brain is currently processing, all at the same time.

This is wonderful and one of the things that sets you apart from other animals. It is also what puts you into the position of "information overload" all too often. You must utilize your wonderful brain to compartmentalize the information and put it in a proper order so that you can operate as efficiently as possible.

The very organization of this book will assist you in learning and, more importantly, retaining the knowledge for your complete success. The best approach to all things safety and survival in the wilderness is the following list. Please pay close attention to the order of these ideas:

1. Mind-set
2. Skills
3. Tactics
4. Gear

Let me explain why this order is so vital to the topic of survival. During my research over the past several years, I have come across a number of "success" stories related to survival. One distinct common thread in all of them is that those people had a will to survive. This is what I will call proper mind-set. Many of these people had it from previous training, others by sheer good fortune. What you will find in this book are stories of those who did not have success. Many of them had great skills and gear. These two items are what the vast majority of survival hobbyists spend their time on. You need to be different. You need to learn from those with successful mind-sets and also add the skills, tactics and gear. This will provide you with the whole system of learning, practice and preparation.

If you are like most people, you want to go right to the gear, thinking that if you get just the right knife, pack or weapon that you will be just fine. Nothing could be further from the truth. That is exactly why I have included the stories at the front of each chapter. You will notice a common theme within them. Humans are capable of incredible things when they set their minds to it. They are also capable of making poor decisions under stress and being dependent upon gear rather than becoming more self-reliant. The key is knowing how to set your mind to it.

The proven method is to keep things simple. By keeping things simple and in a logical order, you can then set your brain up for success. Remember that one of the things that sets your brain apart from other animals is that you have multiple processors taking in and processing information. There is a time and place for you to turn those processors off or to focus your attention on certain thoughts rather than letting them run rampant inside your cranium.

I want you to understand that our proven methods for safety and survival work and, like all things I do, I keep them simple. Here they are:

KEEP IT SIMPLE. "Keep It Simple, Stupid" (KISS), comes in great here. Do not entangle your brain processors on too many tasks at once. I use the principle of "Stop, Think, Observe, Plan, Act" (STOPA) to accomplish this.

KNOW WHAT YOUR BODY NEEDS. Note that I did not say what your body *wants*, but what it *needs*. This is vitally important to your continued improvement in these topics. To simplify this, I use what is referred to as the Rule of Three. (Note that this Rule of Three is different than the critical or combat Rule of Three discussed earlier.)

THINK CREATIVELY BUT DO NOT UNNECESSARILY TRY TO REINVENT THE WHEEL. Many things in survival training are done, particularly on TV, to make the person stand out. For true survival practical application, you need to survive—nothing more and nothing less.

The United States military devised simple methods of using physical skills after years of research and trials. They are proven to be effective. Let's dig into this first one. Presume you are under stress because you have taken the wrong trail, overcorrected and are now lost. What do you do? How do you handle it? This is where STOPA comes into play.

To *stop*, you should literally sit down and stop what you are doing. When under stress, you have any number of physiological processes going on that will limit your ability to think clearly—narrowing of your vision, auditory exclusion, high blood pressure, adrenaline dump and much more. If you take the time to sit down and stop, you can then allow your body to calm back down so that you can think clearly. There is evidence available that shows simply stopping and breathing will reboot the nervous system and calm the body (I will cover this in detail in Chapter 5).

Next, *think* about what you have in your possession that can help you stay alive. What is in your pockets, in your pack, in your vehicle (if you have one) that can assist you in meeting your needs?

After you have taken the time to think, you will probably note some things are missing. You will then need to *observe* your surroundings and start to take, or build, what you are missing from the area.

Once you have stopped, thought and observed, you need to make a *plan* with that information. Most often, you are best served by letting others come find and assist you. In some situations, you will need to self-rescue (I will help you discern which is better later). Stick with your plan, but also prepare contingencies for various situations.

Finally, you need to *act* in order to stay alive. I do not mean that you must physically keep doing something. That will only serve to use up hydration and burn up needed calories. What I do mean is that you must *mentally* stay alive, keep your mind active and do not let it wander to self-pity or things that will make your situation worse. Stick with your plan.

STOPA

STOP: Sit Down

THINK: Consider what you have

OBSERVE: Observe your surroundings

PLAN: Make a plan of success

ACT: Actively keep your mind alert

RULE OF THREE

THREE MINUTES FOR AIR AND BLOOD: You cannot live more than three minutes without oxygen/blood flow continuing in your body.

THREE HOURS FOR CORE BODY TEMPERATURE: You cannot live more than three hours without maintaining your core body temperature.

THREE DAYS FOR HYDRATION: You cannot live more than three days without maintaining or obtaining hydration for your body.

THREE WEEKS FOR FOOD: You cannot live more than three weeks without the energy you derive from eating food.

THREE MONTHS FOR COMPANIONSHIP: Around the three-month mark, the typical person will start to experience depression, anxiety or similar emotional issues without companionship. It is incredibly important to work with others whenever possible rather than going it alone.

I would like to make sure you know that these fundamental concepts are the same ones that have been passed down from professional survival instructors to their students for many years. In this modern age where everyone sells themselves as an expert, I have come to recognize that some things do not need fixing. Assessing our needs is one. The origins of the Rule of Three (a.k.a. Law of Three) is unknown. It is known that at some point in time, it made its way into a United States military survival manual. In my estimation, there is no other more simplified way of knowing what your needs are under stress.

The Rule of Three is not absolute. This is a general understanding of what your needs are. This also does not take into account outside influences, such as weather. These two well-used methods (STOPA and the Rule of Three) are *the* way to build a foundation that is easily retained and then utilized under stress. By reading and continuing to study the methods of this book, you will develop within you the ability to handle stressful situations.

DEVELOPING SURVIVAL SYSTEMS OF STUDY

The big question that arises is: How do you best study ways that you hope to never use in real life? Much like self-defense training, survival training builds skills that you prep and train for that you realistically may use once or twice in your life—and many people will never need to use them. But, because you *may* need these skills at some point, the obvious answer to the question is to immerse yourself in the training from an early age. Yet many of us find ourselves learning at a more mature age, having never spent much time in a wilderness setting.

If you are new to the idea of survival and preparedness, I commend you for being wise enough to dig in now and learn these methods. If you have children, then by all means include them as well. There is a reason companies make backpack-style child carriers that small children fit into. Get them outside. You will find that typically they are more resilient than you are. This is because they do not know that certain temperatures or conditions are supposed to be "bad." When my children were young, my wife and I committed one weekend a month for one full year (and dozens of other times) to going outside and hiking, backpacking, camping and more. We went no matter what the conditions were the first weekend of every month. Our kids did not really know that it was a "bad" thing that it was raining, they just knew they got to play in puddles and make mud cakes.

If you do not have children or a spouse and you are interested in getting started, then consider yourself no different than a small child. The best time to start is now. Take things slow. Here is a good progression of how this could easily happen:

➡ Visit a nature preserve, park or similar location. Take a lunch from home or buy some on the way to picnic. Get a picnic table and have a nice meal. See what you can see. Pick up some trail brochures. Talk to personnel who work there, if they are available, about what the location has to offer.

➡ Go back to the same park for a short hike. Take your Tier 1 gear with you (see Chapter 15).

➡ Find a hiking club in your area. A good place to start is an outdoor hiking store. Better yet, find a coworker, friend or family member to take you hunting. You do not have to necessarily hunt yourself—just go with them and learn how they do things.

➡ Go to a campground that has bathroom facilities. Learn the laws and regulations of the area. Go camping for a night. Take everything but the kitchen sink. You want to be comfortable.

➡ Continue these camping trips but slowly take facilities and gear away. Emphasis on slowly.

➡ Plan a trip where you leave your car and camp with only what you can carry on your back. Take someone with experience if at all possible.

➡ Start to add primitive skills and primitive gear to your excursions, such as debris huts and leather pouches. Start to study and act like the indigenous culture of your area. You will eventually be able to live off the land.

This book is a part of your learning and I am certainly glad you found it. You should read it for study, and also take it afield as a guide as you practice skills. Follow the chapters in order to help you develop your mind-set, skills, tactics and gear. Please note that this is how you as a human learn new things. You learn by involving yourself with the subject you're trying to master:

SEEING: This is watching someone do something. This can be in person or watching a video.

HEARING: This is hearing someone speak about something. This includes listening to a podcast or reading a book (you are hearing yourself in your head).

DOING: This is you actually getting out, doing the hard skills, taking a class, dealing with environmental conditions and all that goes with it. This last one, doing, is where the "meat and potatoes" comes from. It is not enough to observe others using their skills. You must get out and practice them with your gear. This will tell you the strength and limitations of you and your gear.

In general, 15 percent of your learning should come from seeing, 15 percent from hearing and 70 percent from doing. There is absolutely no better teacher than practical hands-on experience. This includes going to a class like those I teach at Nature Reliance School. However, there is a huge mistake being made by hundreds of people taking skills courses with outdoor-survival training schools (including my own). That mistake is trying to imitate the instructor. While most of these men and women have great skill, you need to develop your own skill, not try to imitate theirs. I am not suggesting that you cannot duplicate their skill level. You certainly can and then some. What I am saying is develop and hone your skill set. A good instructor will develop the best *you* that they can develop, not help to create imitations of themselves.

SURVIVAL PHYSIOLOGY AND WHY IT IS IMPORTANT TO YOUR NEEDS

In a true survival situation, you must come to recognize that your body is a machine and that your brain controls how well or poorly that machine will work.

Like a machine has physics and mechanics to determine how well it works, your physiology dictates how well you will survive. Think of a lawn mower. Crank it up, and you can walk away from it and it will run. It has fuel in it to make it run. What we fail to notice about an engine, as well as our physiology, is that there is a certain amount of protection going on that is often unnoticed.

You must take care of your personal safety first. This sets your body's oxygen and blood apparatuses up to work properly. As those in the military are apt to say, "Play stupid games, win stupid prizes." Take care of yourself and do not take unnecessary risks. This will help your body to shelter these systems that keep your lungs and heart pumping.

RAP—REQUISITE ACTION PLAN

→ **Tell someone where you are going and when you expect to return. This will assist in getting help to you as soon as possible if some crisis situation were to occur.**

→ **Know the area you are traveling, what sort of environmental conditions (e.g., rock slides, rough rapids) or wildlife are in the area that could bring harm to you without any errors being made on your part. Have contingency plans if those things were to occur.**

→ **Take your Tier 1 and Tier 2 gear with you. This will include supplies for personal safety, first aid, thermoregulation and hydration. You'll learn all this in great detail in Chapter 15.**

→ **Check the weather before you go. Make necessary preparations should the weather dictate them (i.e., extra layers, rain jackets).**

Do a quick study of wilderness situations that ended with death and the statistics will not lie to you. Most fatalities in the wilderness are due to exposure. Exposure is the technical, one-word way of saying that the person did not regulate their body temperature correctly. Whether they became separated from their gear or they did not have the correct gear to begin with is unimportant to this situation. You must be very cognizant of the weather before you go outside and have plans if the weather goes awry.

Personal safety and core body thermoregulation should be your main focus when going into any wilderness setting. You will have a few days to deal with additional problems if they arise. Therefore, understanding that your physiology demands it, review the Requisite Action Plan (RAP) box above before you go out.

Follow these few suggestions and you should be prepared if something were to happen within a relatively short period of time of you going into the wilderness.

Now that you have the foundation of these all-important systems of study, the next step is to develop your mind-set to both keep you safe from harm and ready to deal with difficult circumstances should they arise. Our first topic will be to make sure you are more aware of your surroundings.

CHAPTER 2

METHODS TO INCREASE AWARENESS OF YOUR SURROUNDINGS

KNOWING IS NOT ENOUGH, WE MUST APPLY. WILLING IS NOT ENOUGH, WE MUST DO.

—JOHANN WOLFGANG VON GOETHE

So much has been written and explored about Christopher McCandless (see the book and movie titled *Into the Wild*) that there is no need for this story to be about an anonymous person. McCandless walked into the Alaskan bush on an idealistic trip to find himself. Many weeks later he was found dead from starvation. The root of this starvation is still hotly debated. It may have been due to his inadequacy to provide for his needs in that environment or a native seed that caused digestion issues.

What is known, however, is that McCandless, at one point in his adventure, determined that he was ready to leave and either travel back home or continue on his traveling ways. When he did so, he found that a river he had crossed on his way into the bush was at flood stage from spring thaw and glacial melt.

It was at this point in his trip that he turned around and traveled back to his shelter and was forced to stay longer than he had determined. This led to his demise, starved and alone.

There are a number of things that went wrong, based upon poor decision making, that caused McCandless to perish alone in the Alaskan bush. Let's focus on the topic at hand and consider only those that deal with awareness of your surroundings.

When crossing over or near a river or stream, note the high-water marks. You can easily see these marks by noting leftover debris. When a river, creek or similar body of water rises, wood, trash and other leftovers will often be suspended at the highest level the water reached. Additionally, most wooded undergrowth and vegetation will grow outside of this high-level mark. This could assist you in making appropriate decisions for a seasonal rise of water or simply a flash flood from heavy rains. You should never find yourself setting up a camp, building a fire or conducting a similar activity anywhere near or below the high-water marks. You should also note each time you cross a stream that if there were heavy rains, it will most certainly be a different crossing when you come back to it.

McCandless also did not take any sort of map. Had he done so, he could have easily seen on a basic topography map that he was only a short hike from a government water-level monitoring station, one which spanned the river even at flood stage. He could have easily crossed that station and made his way back to civilization.

Here is a positive example of utilizing awareness that comes from my own outdoor experiences. A friend and I went on an overnight canoe trip. He and I went on this trip during some spring rains because it was the only time that the water of that particular river was high enough to paddle. We set up our camp far from the river but left the canoe tied to a tree on the riverbank with our paddles secured to it.

It rained incredibly hard that night and the water of that particular river is known to rise very quickly. When daylight hit, we discovered our camp was fine, as well as the canoe. However, the canoe, which was on the riverbank when we went to bed, was floating on about 10 feet (3 m) of water. The river had risen that quickly in the night. Thankfully, we had noted the high-water marks and the weather that was coming our way and had therefore tied it to a tree. If we hadn't done so, it would have floated away and we would have literally been up a creek without a paddle (or canoe).

Awareness of your surroundings is vitally important to not only your safety and survival but also to the increased value of your day-to-day life. It is no secret that with so many handheld electronic devices playing a huge role in most everyone's daily life, there is a huge gap in many people's awareness of their surroundings. This is often referred to as situational awareness rather than self-awareness. Self-awareness is an incredibly in-depth topic, diving into such weighty topics as who we are, levels of consciousness and much more. We will touch on those subjects a bit more when we dig into Chapter 4.

I want to focus your attention on situational awareness for good reason. Humans have a tendency to take in, yet ignore, their surroundings. We definitely have the physical components to be aware of our surroundings through our senses of sight, touch, hearing, smell and, to a lesser degree, even taste. These are all designed to make us aware of what is going on outside of our own bodies. Our minds know that the things that bring immediate danger come from external influences. In the modern world, many have unfortunately taught themselves to not pay attention to these external indicators. I want to help you turn those back on. I also want to help you turn on the ability to be more in control of your mind. What you'll learn in this chapter will assist you in paying more attention to what is going on around you at any given time. More importantly, by paying attention to those things, you will learn how to make good decisions based upon the external factors affecting you at any given point.

There are three very useful techniques that you can use to develop your awareness:

1. Your sit spot

2. KIMs game

3. Decision making

YOUR SIT SPOT

I first heard of the name "sit spot" when I was going through naturalist training with the Wilderness Awareness School. The founder of that school, Jon Young, was a pioneer in many ways of taking people who were new to the outdoors and helping them to be more situationally aware.

At its core, this activity is nothing more than finding a spot in a place to see wild things and then simply sitting there. This method is good for all of us, even those who live in an urban setting. However, to get the most out of your training, it would be best to find a wilder area. A forest, park or stream would work well, but even a bird feeder hung outside your window can help you get started on the right foot.

The purpose of such an exercise is to simply start to see patterns. The natural surroundings seem random and without order. However, there is an incredible amount of order that can be quantified if you take the time to investigate and study it. Here are the steps I recommend to start developing your awareness:

Sketching is an integral part of studying the outdoors.

➡ Find a spot as far from human interaction as possible. Pick a spot that you can go to every day, which is ideal. For many of us, this is not possible. The key is to regularly schedule time to do this sort of activity. Even if the time you can allow yourself is only once per month.

➡ Go to that spot and sit there and observe what goes on around you.

➡ Write in a journal each day what you are experiencing. Include anything that stands out to you about your sit each day.

- Sketch things whenever possible. Just keep in mind that the most important aspect of this is observation and awareness with your senses. Sketching helps retain the information you take in through your senses. Remember the file cabinet from Chapter 1? By observing and then sketching, you help to fill up the folders of your mind.

- Do this for 15–30 minutes a day for one month (the ideal). Again, give it as much time as your schedule will allow.

After doing this, review your notes. You will most likely have some of the patterns in your head, but you may notice even more once you review your notes. Here are some examples of things I have noticed when dedicating specific time to doing this:

- Birds start becoming vocally active approximately ten minutes before the sun breaks the horizon.

- Opossums and skunks travel back to their nesting area shortly after daybreak.

- Whitetail deer are more likely to scent me if I am upwind of them.

- Dew stays on ferns longer than on most other vegetation around them.

These are some incredibly simple yet good observations of what was occurring around me. You do not have to choose the same time frame I did. You can choose any portion of the day. There are always things going on in nature. It will also serve you well if, once you complete an initial 30-day sit, you do it again at a different time or maybe even during a different season of the year.

After many times of doing this activity, you can then begin to see patterns of movement of wildlife, plant growth and your interaction with it. This will serve you well in any future survival-related event. In an event, it can be easy to miss resources that are available to you. By practicing these methods, you will start developing an ability to see more resources no matter what situation you find yourself in.

Remember to sketch as many things as you can. Once you take the time to "capture" as much detail as you can in a sketch, you have purposely committed to memory that which you have drawn. If you are like me when I first started, you will say to yourself, "I cannot draw." Please know that you do not have to be good at it. You simply need to attempt it. These sketches are for no one other than yourself (unless you otherwise choose to share). Sketching forces you to notice details.

From my experience tracking animals for over 40 years and training with a number of notable tracking instructors, there is one thing that I've learned you must do to be a good tracker: sketch tracks. The end goal in all of the practices included here is to develop the ability to recognize details. It is rare that a full track, plant species or other usable resource comes into full view. By teaching yourself to see details, you enable your mind to take in information—even if it is only a partial portion of it.

KIMS GAME

KIM is not some supergenius lady of infinite wisdom that you need to play games with. KIM is simply an acronym for "Keep In Memory." This "game" is taught to military and law enforcement personnel in certain fields (particularly investigation teams) as a means for them to teach their brains how to both file away and recall facts and ideas. It is especially useful for anyone who wants to *see* things more than to simply *look* at them. Seeing is becoming *aware* of something from a visual source, while looking is simply directing one's gaze in a specified direction.

You must do a KIMs game with others. Gather your family together during a game night, or call up one or more friends who are also interested in the outdoors and survival and follow these steps:

➡ Have someone gather approximately 25 small items (about the size of your hand) that are of varying size, shape, color and origin. These items can be natural or man-made. Make sure not to let anyone else see the items yet.

➡ Place those items on the ground and cover them with a blanket, tarp or something that will not allow others to see what is under it.

➡ Have those you are training with stand around those items.

➡ Uncover the items for one minute and ask the other people to take notice of what they see under the covering, but to not share their observations with others. They must only take notes in their mind, not on paper.

Keep-In-Memory game items should be diverse in size, color and use.

➡ Cover the items back up. Take a few minutes to discuss what people saw.

➡ Uncover the items so that everyone can recall what they saw and the things that came out of the discussion.

➡ Repeat this as many times as you have items and time for.

➡ Once this has been done, you can then ask others who understand how it works to lead it. In this manner, you will be able to continue your practice of this skill set as well.

Some recommendations to make this more worthwhile is to put in a few items that have a similar color; place an item or two that will be foreign to most everyone (pieces off of a car or appliance work well) and put items that look similar to other household items in the pile.

To improve your ability to retain what you are seeing, follow these helpful hints:

➡ Know how to scan in a *Z* pattern properly, meaning you start at the pile wherever it is closest to you, scan left to right, then scan at a diagonal from right to left, then left to right again. Then scan up and down in the same *Z* pattern. As you are scanning, begin to imprint into your brain what you are seeing.

- Group items that are alike. You may note that there are three orange items, ten items shaped like a tool and four dangerous items. It certainly depends upon the group I am working with, but I will almost always place an empty handgun in the mix with a magazine that is not seated properly. Many people get focused on dangerous items and cannot take in others.

- Once you have done the initial scan and grouping, it is then time to go back and start to get details. What degree of measurement is the compass set on? Is the knife sharp? What kind of weapon is laying there? Is it loaded? These are the sorts of questions I will detail.

A broad look, then focused scan, on important areas will help you to find needed resources.

When you are leading this type of exercise for your training partners, be sure and ask questions during the initial discussion such as, "Why do you think the knife is sharp?" "What makes you think the gun is loaded?" "How do you know that it is the top off of a blender?" What you will discover is that it is experience with items that will make you better at this game.

The question you may be asking yourself is how to apply this to a wilderness setting. Simply put, you can utilize this as a means for a number of things. Here are suggestions:

- Use the *Z* scanning method to scan for tracks, signs or wildlife in an effort to be a better hunter or to find food in a survival situation.

- Use the scanning technique to look through a wilderness (lots of similar items) and pick out trees that are better for fire-starting, those that will help you develop shelter and those that indicate water. You will literally be teaching yourself how *not* to see the forest for the trees.

- By learning how to commit an area to memory, you can then use that information to go back if you should be injured or otherwise need to go home prematurely.

- Utilize the memorization skills to remember bends in trails, trees that stand out, rock formations or other natural features that you can then relay to a search and rescue (SAR) team over the phone to help them find you or in person to help them find others.

CHAPTER 3

INCREASE YOUR ABILITY TO AVOID DANGER

THE AIM OF EDUCATION SHOULD BE TO TEACH US HOW TO THINK, RATHER THAN WHAT TO THINK. TO IMPROVE OUR MINDS, SO AS TO ENABLE US TO THINK FOR OURSELVES, RATHER THAN TO LOAD THE MEMORY WITH THOUGHTS OF OTHER MEN.

—BILL BEATTIE

In the spring of 1996, two good friends went on a very cold and rainy paddling trip down Rockcastle River near Mount Vernon, Kentucky. These two paddlers had years of experience together, going on paddling trips dozens of times over the years. They took great pride in running rivers and creeks with fast-running rapids, huge boulders and keeper hydraulics.

Rockcastle River is a meandering waterway with several miles of flatwater and plenty of smallmouth bass for the taking. Upon reaching what are referred to as the "narrows," the river takes on a completely different demeanor for a few miles before it dumps into a man-made lake at the end. These sorts of waterways are always good to teach a person how to humble themselves, and this trip was determined to do that in a special way.

As soon as the paddlers started going at the rapids, they took on water multiple times and had to jump into the water, bail water out and then pick up gear that was continually getting washed out of the open-deck canoe.

The paddlers finally had enough and decided to pull over for the night, catch a few fish, eat dinner, relax and hit the biggest and worst of the rapids that were to come the following day. They had run this river before. They knew what to expect. They had a good time as they camped near the first big rapid and an eddy just below it, where they caught a few fish for dinner.

Upon rising the next day, they put on their wet clothes and polar fleece jackets due to the low temperature. They promised each another not to dump the canoe and got everything in and ready to go. Due to the chilly air, they determined that instead of scouting the river directly ahead, they would "just hit it." In their minds, they were confident because they had done similar rapids so many times before. They wanted to get going so they could warm up.

In the first rapid they came to, literally within seconds of starting off, the nose of the canoe hung up on a boulder, effectively trapping the boat. The rushing water proved to be too much and folded the canoe literally in half, dumping the paddlers and all their gear into the water.

Paddler One swam to safety on one side of the river. Paddler Two, the one at the nose, got dumped directly into the rapid and was sucked down to the bottom of the rapid where he was tumbled over and over again against rocks, logs and the heavy pressure of the water. This same paddler eventually gave into the pressure and gave up, taking water into his lungs and beginning the process of drowning.

When his body relaxed, the rapid threw him out (whether his deliverance resulted from simple physics or divine intervention is not known). The paddler then regained consciousness and threw himself on a rock to expel the water from his lungs. He gathered his wits, saw that the other paddler had a similar experience and then traveled downstream to gather their gear.

The paddlers had tied their gear in tightly due to the experiences the day before. This proved to be a problem because the canoe was now wrapped around a rock in the middle of the river with no access to it. The two paddlers had to make their way to the parking spot several miles away, cross-country, with wet clothes on their backs and no gear—all while enduring very cold temperatures.

You may be wondering why I might have so much detail on this particular story. Simply put, I am Paddler Two from the story above. This particular event is one of those life-changing events that fortunately turned out for the best. As a matter of fact, the book you are now reading is partly a result of that event. I learned some incredibly valuable lessons. Now is as good a time as any to share them with you.

There is absolutely no debate: ego was the cause of this particular event. My friend and I had been paddling so much leading up to this event that we felt we were unstoppable. We always scouted each and every rapid before we hit it. However, we came unprepared and therefore were cold. We decided to "just hit it" due to our chill, as well as overconfidence in our skills.

We also carried zero gear in our life vests during these trips. We had no knives, no fire-starting equipment and no hydration methods in our vests, which was the only equipment attached to our bodies. That was a huge mistake. You should always carry a knife and fire-starting equipment on you no matter what task you are engaged in. In this particular situation, a lighter would have been soaked and unusable, but with a good ferrocerium rod and something to strike it with (the back of the knife), we could have made ourselves a fire.

The one thing we did do right is that we had a serious discussion about the trip and looked at a map of the area before we got on the river. We determined that up to a certain very discernable point in the river that if something were to occur, we would hit the east side of the river. After that point, we determined that we would hit the west side. In both cases, that side of the river would get us to a trail out in short order.

That is exactly what we did. We hit the west side of the river, walked up the hill until we hit the trail and hiked out to our vehicle. This preplanning probably saved our lives. Had we not determined where we would go in an unexpected event, we would not have even known where to begin. Rockcastle River is a federal wild-protected river, which means there can be no development within a large buffer zone around it. There would have been no one close to us at any point along the trip.

With that said, we did not have compasses or GPS. We knew direction based upon time of day and that the sun rises in the east. This little bit of woods skill comes in handy on a very regular basis. Commit it to memory and always note your direction whenever you plan on going outside.

I am thankful that this event occurred. It, along with many other experiences, directly led to this book. Now that I have more maturity and experience, let me share how you can prevent this sort of thing happening to you.

EGO IS A KILLER

There is a secret killer out there that wants to ride alongside all of us, have internal conversations with us and ultimately kill you if you allow it to. That secret killer is ego.

Ego is a driving force for many. We want to look better, feel better, be stronger and have more woods skills than someone else. What we should be doing is not becoming attached to those sorts of thoughts in the first place.

I am not saying that competition is a bad thing. Having competition in a training environment can work for those who lack the ability to motivate themselves. It is that training that develops the ability to accomplish the tasks that need to be done. To be more clear, you can engage in a friendly competition with a friend on who can build the fastest fire using only material made from the landscape. That does not mean that you are a great fire builder. The lessons to take away from such an activity is what worked well and what did not work well. For the things that did not go well, you need to practice more or find gear pieces that will help until you can become better at the skill.

I have put together a distilled list of the must-have strategies to help you avoid danger. This list is born out of many years of training with some of the best in the world, including Army Special Forces and Rangers, Navy SEALs, Air Force Combat Controllers and even a MARSOC Marine:

- **Avoidance and awareness**
- **Cockiness versus confidence**
- **Own your mistakes and learn from them**
- **Seventy percent accuracy is good enough**
- **Have humility**
- **Understand the Combat Rule of Three**
- **Surround yourself with people better than you**

AVOIDANCE AND AWARENESS

There are certainly wilderness crisis situations that take some completely by surprise. Most, however, could easily be avoided. Common sense can go a long way when dealing with stressful situations in the wilderness. There are times when a number of people have been caught in these situations and foresight said that it was going to happen. You have a keen sense that will alert you to danger—you need to simply listen to that sense and heed its warnings. A river is too swift to paddle; a crevice is too far to jump over; your leader does not know how to read a map—those are all things you could simply avoid. The question that begs to be asked is *how* to avoid them. The simplest way to avoid bad situations is to have the awareness that they are going on. You can see, hear and smell danger in many ways. Acknowledge it, listen to your gut and be aware that your senses are telling you something.

I am not saying that you should never do anything that gets you "charged up," never go into dangerous places and do dangerous things. What I am saying is that awareness that they are dangerous is exactly what you need to have to set yourself up for success. Mission planning is key to any special forces unit. It can also be good for you to plan for such things, as well as contingencies if things go wrong.

COCKINESS VERSUS CONFIDENCE

There is a huge difference between these two demeanors. Cockiness is ego-based and will allow your ego, what I refer to as "the false self," to direct your actions and your words. Confidence is intelligence-based and will also direct your actions and your words but to a much more logical and safer situation. When your ego is driving you, you will simply continue to put yourself in situations that are hard to get through and time will eventually catch up

with you. Ego forces you to be reactive. (Remember my story of running so many rivers that I knew I could run that one rapid that nearly cost us our lives?) When your intelligence drives you, it allows you to be in position to make decisions and to be proactive.

Being proactive means that more often than not, you will have an opportunity to see dangerous or stressful situations before they occur. By doing so you will then be able to assess the situation more clearly and make appropriate decisions. Being reactive puts you in the unseemly position of already being in an unfortunate situation. When you find yourself there, you physiologically cannot make the best decision. Your body will increase your heart rate and blood pressure and provide an adrenaline dump. Your vision and your hearing will decrease considerably. This leads to decisions that are not properly informed, which leads to you putting yourself in worse positions more often than not.

OWN YOUR MISTAKES AND LEARN FROM THEM

No one likes to make mistakes. But high-performing military athletes from special forces will tell you that mistakes are simply part of life, to not get bogged down in them and to take what you can from the mistake and use it for personal, team or family growth.

Again, these military folks are the ones who find themselves in some of most dangerous situations in the world. They make mistakes during training and learn from them, so that when the time comes and their lives depend upon smart decisions, their actions move them forward. In your team or family, you must be vocal with one another on mistakes that cause problems. You do not have to berate someone over their mistakes, but you also cannot simply let them go without everyone learning from them. It is through these mistakes that the whole team or family (or simply the individual) will experience the most growth.

SEVENTY PERCENT ACCURACY IS GOOD ENOUGH

I learned this mind-set from John Hurth, a retired special forces soldier, author of the book *Combat Tracking Guide* and lead instructor of TÝR Group. I took one of many man-tracking courses under John's guidance and instruction. There is a mind-set with those in tactical-related skill sets that states you must get past the "paralysis by analysis" situation (which is when you assess a situation so much that you either get bogged down in details or by the situation itself and get nowhere). In the class, Hurth told us to assess a man-tracking situation up to 70 percent accuracy and move on from it. It was the first time I had this practice put in such quantifiable terms. It actually assisted me and the team I was on in getting a lot more work done. If you see a situation arising and you need to assess, do not get bogged down in all the details. Simply get 70 percent of them completed and then move on from there.

HAVE HUMILITY

This can easily be seen in those that have better listening skills than speaking skills. In many conversations, most people will only half-listen to what is going on around them because they are thinking of what they are going to say next and looking for a window to interject. Listening skills are more important than speaking skills to keep you out of these stressful and dangerous situations. It could be as simple as listening and watching for signs of dehydration in someone in your family or team (or even yourself). Humble yourself to listen to people and not assume that they have the fortitude, or even the ability, to recognize they are having issues.

UNDERSTAND THE COMBAT RULE OF THREE

In battle, like in a survival situation, you need to make decisions under stress. It is difficult for many to make decisions under such conditions. You will often freeze and "lock up." This method of decision making is designed for the purpose of getting you out of the locked-up position you may find yourself in. The application for survival situations is that if you recognize three instances of anything out of the ordinary, you should change what you are doing. For example, if you are going for a day hike and you realize you have forgotten your map (instance number one), you should make note of it for certain, make decisions about it and possibly continue your trek. If, however, you also realize you did not bring any water (instance number two) *and* it looks like unexpected bad weather (instance number three), you should then change what you are doing. Think of the Combat Rule of Three as being akin to "three strikes and you are out," to use a sports analogy.

SURROUND YOURSELF WITH PEOPLE BETTER THAN YOU

This is not always possible for events, but you should utilize this in preparation and training before an event. I actually learned this lesson from a special forces soldier who was attending a class I was teaching. You may notice that I hold military personnel in high regard. I especially consider those in the special operations community to be some of the most well-trained, high-functioning teams and personnel on the planet. This includes their survival training. However, this special forces soldier attended a class I was teaching in Kentucky. I asked him why he was attending such a basic class. In my mind, he already had the skills. His response both humbled and enlightened me. It was his opinion that I was a subject matter expert in the area of wilderness survival of that region of the world. He therefore wanted to train with me to get more knowledge on the subject since he had recently been stationed at Fort Campbell and was new to the area. He wanted to surround himself with people better than him. Now I do not pretend to know more than even your average special forces soldier. Again, their skills and training are some of the best in the world. Regarding that particular region, for those skills, I did have more in the way of training and experience. He therefore took what he learned from me and applied it to his work.

As I have mentioned before, most survival training is reactive rather than proactive. I want you to be better than that. I want you to spend *more* time outside. By taking the time to follow these simple suggestions, you can do exactly that. I would like to summarize this whole list of positive initiatives by reminding you to be humble. I am not saying you should have a feeling of insignificance or inferiority. I am saying that you need to remember to be confident but that you should also work *with* the environment rather than against it. The resources are there for you to use. The topography and nature of the outdoors have a number of dangers, but only if you try to abuse or inappropriately use them.

A perfect example is that of venomous snakebites in the wilderness. According to herpetology experts, prior to the 1990s, 70 percent of all venomous snakebites occurred below the knee. Although they were rare, this occurred because people were not aware and inadvertently stepped too close to a venomous snake and were bit. After the mid-1990s, there was huge shift in these bites. Now, 70 percent of venomous snakebites occur below the elbow (between the elbow and the hand). Why, you ask? Because of the popularity of TV shows in which various popular personalities handle venomous snakes. People tend to want to imitate art, and they do so without training on proper handling skills.

By remaining humble, you can "enjoy the view" without endangering yourself or taking unnecessary risks. Remember the story at the beginning of this chapter? It is my story. I still paddle that same river and that same rapid that I nearly lost my life in. I simply scout it better, have some better gear and develop a better plan when doing it. By following the simple steps outlined in this chapter, you do not have to avoid danger altogether. Be intelligent in your approach and do not throw caution to the wind.

With that in mind, sometimes accidents and unexpected events do occur. Due to that element of uncertainty, I want you to increase your own mental fortitude to handle those sorts of situations in the next chapter.

CHAPTER 4

DEVELOP YOUR MENTAL FORTITUDE SO THAT YOU CAN HANDLE ANYTHING

RANGER SCHOOL DID NOT TEACH ME HOW TO BE TEN FEET TALL AND BULLETPROOF. IT TAUGHT ME HOW TO RECOGNIZE THAT I WAS REACHING MY LIMITS, BOTH MENTALLY AND PHYSICALLY, AND THEN MAKE THE APPROPRIATE ADJUSTMENTS WITH MYSELF AND MY TEAM TO ACCOMPLISH THE TASK AT HAND.

—PARAPHRASE OF COMMENTS MADE BY A U.S. ARMY SPECIAL FORCES SOLDIER

For many years, Ranger school proved to be some of the most demanding training offered in the United States military. Ranger candidates go through various phases of training to earn the coveted Ranger tab. One such phase often takes place in the swamps of Florida. It was there that tragedy struck for the Rangers.

From published accounts of the incident in 1995, it was revealed that several Ranger candidates were nearing the completion of Ranger training. After a morning boat exercise, they had been tasked to enter the water and build some rope bridges. This particular area of water was deeper than it normally had been in the past. For much of this exercise, the candidates were in waist-deep (and sometimes chest-deep) water. The 52°F (11°C) water temperature was nearing the bottom threshold of 50°F (10°C) required for training to be cancelled. The air temperature was in the 60s Fahrenheit (in the 10s Celsius), meaning this was a situation where hypothermia was very possible.

That is exactly what happened to several candidates that day. Ranger instructors recognized that hypothermia was setting in for some of them. A decision was made to extract several of the candidates showing signs of hypothermia, such as uncontrollable shaking, slurred speech and loss of fine motor skills. Unfortunately for four of them, it was too late and they died of hypothermia-related issues.

I would be out of line to second-guess the Ranger instructors on this situation, especially since I hold Ranger instructors in very high regard. With that said, there is one incredibly valuable lesson you can learn from this tragedy.

All special operations personnel in the United States military, such as these candidates, are known to have what many would consider superhuman mind and body control. They overcome obstacles that many consider impossible. But the cold, hard facts are that the human body has limits. The key to surviving harsh environments is to recognize when you are in a situation where you are nearing those limits. Better yet, recognize a situation that could lead to those limits being pushed and plan accordingly.

Preparing for war is similar to an actual war in that it is an ugly, convoluted mess of exercises that will sometimes lead to someone's death. For special operations personnel, that is a hazard of the job. For the rest of us, you can stay mentally and physically strong as well. You must recognize your limits and make changes when you are reaching them.

There is no shortage of research that has been done regarding mental strength and resiliency. The United States Army started its own program involving such research and established the Comprehensive Soldier and Family Fitness Program in 2008. While this is specific to the U.S. military, I have had many opportunities to speak to soldiers and their families on this topic. I have listened intently and adapted these practices to our needs in survival. The Army considers five distinct aspects of our lives when assisting soldiers in helping them achieve mental strength: physical, social, family, spiritual and emotional. It is worthy of our consideration to understand these various aspects of our lives and how they play out in our resiliency. To make it easier to understand and directly applicable, I have developed a list of ways to help you both overcome obstacles and increase the strength of your mind:

- Constantly improve yourself
- Recognize and release tension
- Be flexible
- Have a purpose
- Believe you are strong
- Have a sense of humor
- Stay positive
- Be healthy
- Be organized
- Work on your relationships

CONSTANTLY IMPROVE YOURSELF

Self-assessment is critical to self-improvement. You must regularly consider what you need to improve upon. If you have standards or foundations for character, work and other aspects of your life, you can then consider them and see if you are living up to the standards you set. As I stated in the last chapter, learn from your mistakes. Also, extend this into constant improvement of whatever you endeavor to do. Improve your running times, make a healthier and tastier spaghetti, get more organized. Whatever the task, continue to assess yourself and improve.

RECOGNIZE AND RELEASE TENSION

For the individual, the warning signs are evident. Tight muscles, headaches, poor decision making and more. When you recognize this tension in yourself or someone in your group, you must act soon to make a change. This can be as simple as doing some stretching and breathing (see Chapter 5) or as deep as sharing responsibilities with someone else.

BE FLEXIBLE

The United States Marine Corps is famous for saying, "Adapt, improvise and overcome." Being able to adapt and improvise is born out of being flexible. When you are flexible in your thinking, you come to decisions more clearly. When things are done more clearly, better thoughts and actions can take place.

HAVE A PURPOSE

I am not a huge fan of movie and TV show survival edutainment. However, the movie *Castaway*, starring Tom Hanks, depicted one of the best demonstrations of how to have a purpose that I have seen in a movie showing survival. If you have not seen it, Tom Hanks is a FedEx employee who is on a plane that crashes into the ocean. He is left stranded on an island for several years. One of the things that becomes his focus is making sure that he delivers one of the packages that washed up on the shore of the island. It gives him a purpose to stay alive. You must do that, too. You should have a purpose to stay alive. Someone you love to get back to, an important job, unfinished work at home—whatever you can put into your mind that will help you endure hardships and make you want to work toward staying alive and getting back to normalcy.

BELIEVE YOU ARE STRONG

You must believe you are stronger than the situations you find yourself in. Pain is temporary; it is there to remind you that you are alive. You need to visualize that you are stronger and see yourself successfully navigating the situation that you are in. If you see yourself as strong, it will allow you to conquer the task that needs to be conquered, even if that task is nothing more than gathering firewood when you are cold and hungry. You must believe you are strong. A good practice to get into *before* you need this skill is to spend some extra time listening to motivating speeches. Many people use them (me included) to work out. This helps increase your mental strength. Once you get in the habit of doing this for a workout, you can then use that mind-set in virtually any situation.

HAVE A SENSE OF HUMOR

It takes more muscles to frown than it does to laugh. Laughing at yourself and your situation at times will allow you to not get too focused on the negative side of the situation. If something is funny, laugh at it and share the laugh with others. Your body and mind will appreciate you for it.

STAY POSITIVE

Getting negative is much like getting on a road with two deep ruts where your tires go. It is excessively hard to get back on the good path. Do what you can to stay positive so you do not have this issue.

BE HEALTHY

One of the things I have learned by working with top military and law enforcement units is to do your best to stay in shape. I have a T-shirt that I work out in that reminds me of this. It has a quote on it credited to Tim Kennedy, who is both a decorated former special forces operator and UFC champion. He said, "Every time you train, train with the motivation and purpose that you will be the hardest person someone ever tries to kill." You should not wait to get in shape—the time is now. Once you are in the midst of a survival event, you want to be in the best shape you can be to address the multitude of physical issues you will face.

BE ORGANIZED

Do you remember the *A* in STOPA? *A* means *act* to stay alive, particularly in your mind. One of the best ways to do this is to keep things organized. When preplanning events, get your gear ready and stored properly. In the middle of an event, just simply organizing the firewood into categories by size or type will help you keep your mind active and not burn too many calories.

WORK ON YOUR RELATIONSHIPS

I have done an incredible amount of challenge course facilitation. This work has allowed me to assist groups in quite a range of work and industry to become more productive and efficient. This work has included special forces teams and corporate entities. There are a few things that come from this work that will assist you in working with others. I use the outstretched left hand as a demonstration of these pieces. When working with a group, I will have everyone hold their left hand out and speak of how each finger represents an aspect of positive relationships. Here are those aspects:

LITTLE FINGER: This is the smallest and easiest to break. Regarding relationships, it serves as a reminder to stay safe, to not take unnecessary risks and that relationships are fragile.

RING FINGER: This is the finger you place your wedding band on, which is a reminder of the importance of commitment. Being committed to those in your group or family is imperative. It is not just about you.

MIDDLE FINGER: This finger usually represents disrespect, but I will reverse the meaning of this one to serve as a reminder that I will respect others at all times. I will focus my attention on the situation and not on the person.

PRIMARY FINGER: This finger is usually used to point at others and be accusatory. If you hold your hand up and point at someone else, you will notice that you also have three other fingers pointing at yourself, which means you need to assess yourself and your actions rather than accusing others.

THUMB: I am sure you know it already. It represents a "thumbs-up" attitude. Do what you can to stay positive. Have a great attitude and work with others.

These are also ways I help others to become a more cohesive team at work. They will help you to be proactive rather than reactive. They will serve you well to stay out of danger and to make better decisions during an unexpected event. There is no greater need to work as a team than in a survival situation.

I have considered many aspects of handling stressful events up to this point. I also want to help you develop the ability to reassess what is considered stress in the first place. If certain events are no longer stressful at all, it will help you to address them from a more balanced position. In that regard, I will cover mindfulness in the next chapter.

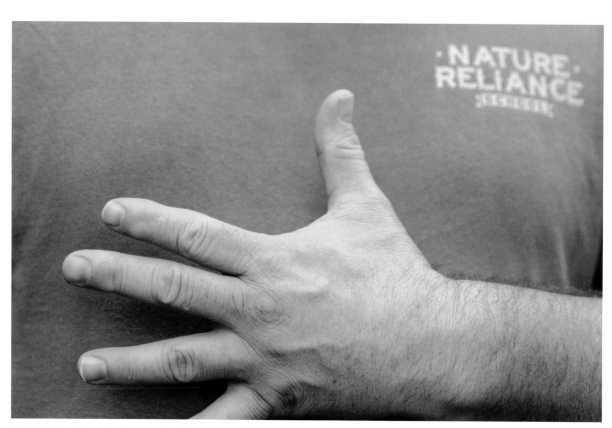

The hand is used as a simple reminder of how to communicate effectively.

CHAPTER 5

MINDFULNESS AND TRANSFORMING YOUR PERSPECTIVE ON EVERYTHING YOU ENCOUNTER

MINDFULNESS MEANS PAYING ATTENTION IN A PARTICULAR WAY; ON PURPOSE, IN THE PRESENT MOMENT AND NONJUDGMENTALLY.

—JON KABAT-ZINN

I first heard of the following story when reading Allan Eckert's *The Frontiersmen* many years ago. The story goes that the great Shawnee warrior Tecumseh had a vision that he was going to die at the Battle of Thames. Due to this, he had some words of encouragement for those under his leadership. One of his close supporters was told that if Tecumseh was downed in battle, all he had to do was strike him with his ramrod three times and Tecumseh would rise from the dead.

Prior to this battle, Tecumseh had formed an amalgamation of native people to go against the United States. He had incredible power in convincing them because he had foreseen events that actually occurred. One in particular he prophesied many months in advance, the New Madrid earthquake. This quake, which Tecumseh prophesied to the exact day, is the largest known quake to hit the North American continent.

The battle with the whites led by General William Henry Harrison was a huge defeat for the British and their Native American allies led by Tecumseh. Tecumseh himself was killed at the battle and did not rise from the dead.

A modern movie about Navy SEALs, *Act of Valor*, shared the following quote attributed to Tecumseh: "When your time comes to die, be not like those whose hearts are filled with fear of death, so that when their time comes they weep and pray for a little more time to live their lives over again in a different way. Sing your death song, and die like a hero going home."

I did not share this story to encourage you to become some sort of prophet. This story demonstrates how someone who is mindful handles the eventuality that we must all face: death.

This notion of mindfulness must be in place to do two very important things. One is to help see more of what is going on around you. All people who have lived "close to the earth" have an awareness and sense that many others do not have. For those that live in busy neighborhoods or large cities, you can still cultivate this same sense through mindfulness training. Second, many of us live in fear when our own death is considered. By cultivating the idea of mindfulness, you can overcome that fear and simply live.

Mindfulness is one of those topics that gets tossed to the side for the more attractive, sexier side of survival training (namely, gear and its role in the puzzle). There is a reason that the U.S. military has actively engaged special forces personnel in meditation training from time to time for nearly 30 years. Meditation leads to mindfulness, which leads those who practice it to become more aware of themselves and what is going on around them.

You know that physical strength is something you can achieve by regular and systematic work such as weight lifting or regular body-weight work. What many do not know is that you can also increase your mental strength and toughness through mindfulness training as well.

This fitness of the mind is no different than muscles being strong and fit. With a fit mind that is relaxed, you can more clearly and calmly address situations as they arise as well as better deal with the physiological issues that confront you when you are stressed.

The big question is how do you tap into such training? It is quite easy and I will consider it in four different ways:

1. Breathing

2. Centering

3. Attachment

4. Visualization

I will consider each of these and how to do them properly, as well as address how well they work with safety and survival.

BREATHING

Breathing is one of those actions that you do without thought. Since you began reading this chapter, you have not once told yourself to take a breath. However, breathing in a way that is more efficient and stronger is something that is not easy to do. As a matter of fact, when you are born you breath properly. Stresses placed in our lives lead us to stop doing it. Take a moment to watch a baby (or even your pet) breathing, and you will notice something interesting. I refer to it as "belly breathing."

You must first note that your lungs, which are closer to your back than your front, also extend nearly down to your waist. When you breathe, you usually breathe in such a way that you do not use the full capacity of your lungs. You take shallower breaths than you are capable of. If you breathe properly, you should easily see your abdomen rising as you take a breath in and then lowering as you exhale. We typically hold our stress in our shoulders and neck area and this is the leading reason we have so many headaches. If you learn to relax your shoulders and focus your breathing in such a way that you can see the proper change in your abdomen, you are doing well.

From a physiological standpoint, you are simply insuring that there is more oxygen coming into your body, which in turn provides oxygen to your blood, which in turn shares it with your musculature and brain. By doing so you are effectively giving your entire body more of the vital elements that it needs to operate properly.

AN EXERCISE IN MINDFULNESS

Find a location where you can be away from major distractions.

- ➡ **Find a place to sit comfortably. Pay attention that your head and spine are erect; do not slouch.**

- ➡ **Place your hands on your abdomen so that you can feel yourself breathe.**

- ➡ **When you inhale, you should feel your hands rise.**

- ➡ **When you exhale, you should feel your hands lower.**

- ➡ **Do your best to not think about anything in particular; rather, allow your thoughts to enter your mind and just as quickly leave your mind without consideration.**

Practice this exercise for fifteen minutes each day. Increase it by five-minute increments until you can comfortably do this for 30 minutes each day. The benefits of this practice are proven: improved circulation, more oxygenated blood flow, increased performance of the lymphatic system, clearer thinking, less stress. This is exactly what you need to think clearly. When thinking clearly, you can then formulate plans, work on skills and do the other things that will help you to not only survive but do so as easily as possible.

PHYSIOLOGICAL CHANGES DUE TO SURVIVAL STRESS

- Increase in heart rate
- Rapid breathing
- Auditory exclusion
- Reduced blood flow to extremities
- Minimized vision (tunnel vision)

In any given survival situation, you must consider the importance of this. When you get excessively stressed, your body has a range of physiological changes it goes through.

Once these things begin to occur, our decision-making process is poor. The information you need to make decisions is limited due to your senses. Your thought process is rambling because of the external influences that are wreaking havoc at any given time. The key to fixing these problems is your breathing. Simply breathe. Breathing immediately turns the switch on for these systems, telling them to get back to normal.

CENTERING

Centering is simply the act of bringing balance back to both your body and your mind. Many are aware that there is a direct connection between mind-body unification and sports figures that are at the top of their game. How can you achieve the same success when you are under stress? You can do that with centering.

Think of it this way: Imagine you are standing with good posture, legs slightly bent, your head straight and your arms relaxed at your side, and I hand you a five-pound (2.3-kg) medicine ball. You will quickly place the ball

next to your core. This is your wheelhouse of power and where it will be rather easy for most everyone to simply hold onto that weight. Imagine again that you are standing on one leg, leaning to your right side, with your right arm stretched out. I then place that same five-pound (2.3-kg) ball in your hand and ask you to hold it. You can probably see yourself struggling with it, even if it is only slightly so. Your support muscles will have enough problem keeping you from falling. When the ball is placed in your hand, your muscles are even more stressed. While you are attempting to stay balanced and hold the ball up you will find it is harder to make decisions because your conscious and subconscious mind is simply trying to not fall or drop the ball. That is a look at the extremes of being centered versus not being centered.

Now consider this in the case of survival. If you are running in disarray, moving from one task to the next without regard to posture and control, you simply cannot make mindful decisions or considerations. This does not mean that you must walk around in some particularly posture-perfect position. It might mean that you actually take time to sit down and consider what is going on in the situation. Remember in the first chapter I discussed

STOPA and how the *S* represented *stop* and even *sit down*? Taking the time to center yourself each day is an incredibly important practice.

I do not mean that you must sit in some meditative posture (although that sort of practice *is* rewarding). What I mean is take time to sit comfortably on the ground or in a chair and simply gather your thoughts each day. The reason I suggest this for each day is because this is another preemptive way to get ready for stressful situations that come with survival.

Your brain has a number of neuropathways that connect centers of thought (think of them as thought highways). You might have a thought about something and a solution for it in another part of your brain. However, a neuropathway has not been built to connect the two. Once those pathways are built, thoughts can travel through them and do so more efficiently. If you spend a portion of each day in centered breathing practice, you will increase the number of these pathways that will guide solutions to your problems. You simply begin to think more clearly. Once you find yourself in a survival situation, those pathways are then built. Center yourself in the midst of the stress, even if it is only in your mind, and things will become clearer and answers will be found.

You may be thinking that this sounds too "different" to you and possibly bordering on the religious side of the topic. All the great religions of the world do certainly have a few things in common. One is that they all share some sort of opportunity for the believer to quietly reflect on situations and to find help with problems. Whether that help comes from God or from within is best left to the individual person to determine. People from all walks of life and from all over the world have proven that this centered way is the best way to make decisions.

ATTACHMENT

It is a simple question with a not-so-simple answer. What are you attached to? A particular knife, a way of life, a person, a job? Attachment and nonattachment are useful traits to have when it comes to wilderness safety and survival.

You can think of attachment in a positive sense as reasons to live. I often read and hear survival stories of how people survived due to something or someone they wanted to stay alive for. Maybe it was a spouse, a child, a job or something much greater or much less. Whatever the case, maybe there was something in their mind that gave the person a reason to live. On the flip side of this: Is there something you are attached to that if you simply let go, you would still be just fine in a survival situation? Some obvious thoughts come to mind:

- → A purse and its contents during a physical assault
- → The idea that people will look down on you if you fail
- → The inner voice that tells you to give up
- → Situations that do not go your way

The practice should include you being in control of your thought processes. These are busy times in our modern world. What I want you to do in this practice is recognize that this constant busyness is an improper mind-set and do something about it. I am not recommending you "empty your mind." What I am suggesting is that you simply allow thoughts to enter, do not become attached to them and then let them slip away.

VISUALIZATION

Visualization is the act of seeing or feeling things that you cannot actually see or feel. Watch videos of an Army Ranger stepping to the edge of an airplane and jumping off and you might feel butterflies at the magnitude of what they are seeing and doing. How does that work? You were not there; you did not actually see the ground rushing up to greet them as they pulled the parachute. How is it that you can feel as if you are part of it? Simply put, the mind is a very powerful tool. It is no different than dreaming. With visualization, you have more control of the thoughts and visuals you are seeing in your mind. There are three very important considerations to overcome for use in survival situations:

1. Temperature

2. Pain management

3. Fear

TEMPERATURE

In the following chapters, I will be discussing the steps to build shelter and fire, which are both designed to help you either conserve or gain heat. What do you do before you get those completed? What happens if you cannot do those things? You may have to rely upon your mind to help warm you.

The easiest way for most people to practice this is to imagine they are somewhere different than where they actually are. If you are lost, under a tree and surrounded by several feet of snow, you may recognize that the cold is starting to set in. Imagine you are at a beach where you are completely warm and the sun is beating down on you. It is scientifically proven that exercises such as this can change your biochemistry in such a way that the feeling becomes real.

On one trip I was leading, there was a group of special forces soldiers and their sons. I was leading them on a survival training, canoeing, rock climbing and caving trip as a method to help them connect with one another after an extended period of deployment. There are always good stories told around the campfire with men such as these. One such story involved two of these men who had gone through the military's Survival Evasion Resistance and Escape (SERE) school. At one point of the training, the soldiers were given a tarp, stripped to their undergarments and forced to stay the night in subfreezing temperatures surrounded by snow. One of the soldiers explained how he and another soldier put their tarps together, filled them with pine needles and got into them together. They "spooned" to help feed off of one another's body heat, but he also remarked how they visualized that the pine needles were goose down and that they were lying in a remote cabin in a comfy bed. While he was clear that it did not make him comfortable, he most certainly did feel warmer. He credited the visualization process taught by the SERE instructors to be the thing that made the difference.

PAIN MANAGEMENT

Ignoring pain is not a solution to any situation in which you are hurt or injured. The opposite is absolutely true. You must recognize pain for what it is, a signal to your brain that something is wrong. If you have the skill, you need to use your first aid ability and gear to address the pain. Once that is done, or if you do not have first aid skill or supplies, you will need to use your mind to ensure that the pain does not overwhelm you and control you. To do this, you simply consider where the pain is coming from and recognize that pain is caused by your nervous system sending signals to the brain that something is wrong. What you need to do is recognize those signals are there and think of them as something other than pain. It is much like being nonattached to the idea of pain. You disassociate the sensation you are feeling as something negative. Consider it part of you and that you own and control it—it does not control you. In this manner, the pain, which is there, becomes something else entirely.

FEAR

As I write this, there is a multitude of videos circulating through social media that depict cats being scared by their owners who lay a cucumber within a few inches of them while they are unaware. When they see the cucumber it frightens them and they can be seen doing incredible acts of agility and strength to get away from what (I can only guess) they think is a snake. You may know someone like this as well, completely afraid of snakes, spiders, clowns and so on. Fear is real. What we must learn to do is to accept it and utilize it for our own purposes rather than, much like managing pain, allowing it to control us. As the cats so quickly demonstrate, we too can become much stronger, faster and more powerful by embracing fear. I consider it like a brother when I recognize that something wants to scare me. This brother of mine encourages me to become this more powerful being so that I can act accordingly to the situation. Whatever the situation might be, you can then use these newfound powers to address it.

Fear also comes in other ways, however. Fear of injury, fear of sickness, fear of death. I would suggest that this type of fear is there to encourage you to prepare for those things to happen. Are you afraid of an injury, such as falling and breaking your leg? Then visualize

how to handle that situation if it were to occur. Afraid of sickness? Then know what plants you can use for medicine to help thwart it. Afraid of death? Then prepare yourself for the afterlife. If you do not want to do that, then realize if there is nothing after death, you will at least have no worries. If this fear of death is born out of something being left undone, some word being left unsaid, then do not hesitate. Start working on that situation now to correct it.

A teacher of mine once asked me, "If you knew you only had five minutes to live and could call anyone and speak to them and tell them something, who would you call and what would you say?" I am asking you that question right now. Who would you call and what would you say? Then put this book down right now and go do it.

That is the answer to all of these things that cause fear: consider them and how to fix them. Address them now in your mind, so you do not have to address them unprepared in the future.

INCREASING YOUR "TOOLBOX" OF SURVIVAL SKILLS

EVERYONE HAS A PLAN UNTIL THEY GET PUNCHED IN THE FACE.

—MIKE TYSON

Skills are the fun part of survival training as well as proper living. Everyone enjoys building a good fire, right? In this section, I want to delve into the skills you need to stay alive. I am going to show you the skills in order of importance as they relate to the Rule of Three priority scale, which will continue cementing the Rule of Three into your thought processes.

In a world where sporting competitions are a primary source of entertainment, I will focus your attention on skills that consistently work without much technicality. It seems that even in the survival industry, coming up with new and creative ways of doing the most basic of skills is what garners the most attention. I want you to have skills not to impress others but to keep yourself *alive*. I am sharing the most important skills and the ones that can be duplicated under stress. This stress could be an injury (such as a broken arm) or if you have found yourself without gear. That is why I will show multiple ways of doing things with modern gear as well as primitive skills.

In this section, I'll also show you how to get out and practice these skills so you can make them your own. Be on the lookout for the sections titled "Put it into Practice." You'll learn them in such a way that you can combine as many skills as possible to make it realistic training.

CHAPTER 6

TAKING RESPONSIBILITY FOR YOUR PERSONAL SAFETY

SAFETY DOESN'T HAPPEN BY ACCIDENT.
—ANONYMOUS

A young lady and her eleven-year-old son were traveling into Death Valley National Park for the purpose of seeing the sites. She was relying upon her vehicle's GPS to help navigate her way in and out of the park. It is not known whether her GPS gave her a wrong turn or if she took one. She quickly became disoriented and lost. She turned down an unmarked gravel road and her vehicle fell into a caved-in animal burrow and became stuck.

She waited for help but it did not come for five days. After dealing with the excessive heat for so long, the child succumbed to the heat and died. The mother was eventually found by a park ranger and airlifted to a hospital. When found, the vehicle was nearly 10 miles (16 km) from the nearest well-paved, discernible road.

The lessons to be learned here are simple. First and foremost, you should never depend upon anything that requires batteries for your survival. Furthermore, GPS units are notoriously inaccurate. Park rangers have already coined a term in the last decade called "death by GPS" for the multitude of adventure seekers who have gotten lost and died due to a faulty GPS unit.

Beyond that, planning was important in this particular situation. This young lady did have the mind-set to tell people where she was going, but she did not give anyone a time frame. She should have specifically told someone where she was going and when she could be expected home.

She should also have carried supplies with her to navigate without GPS. I carry a map and compass with me every time I get in the car. I leave those in the car for any possible need. Beyond that, she should have understood the area she was traveling and planned for a potential breakdown. This is not a situation where one should simply hope for the best and that is all. You should plan for the worst and hope for the best. By planning ahead, she would have known that she was in an extremely hot area and would need extra water and supplies to shield her and her child from the sun.

When she was found, it was days late and nearly 20 miles (32 km) from her intended destination. She took snacks and drinks for a one-day outing but did not have adequate supplies in case things did not go as planned. Therefore, her child died of a combination of dehydration and heat-related illness.

There are many ways to be responsible for your own actions in a wilderness setting. Let's look at the three that most people assume they can already take care of but in reality usually have little ability to do so: wilderness first aid, land navigation and self-defense.

WILDERNESS AND REMOTE FIRST AID

I would like to begin this section by stating that the best way to train in first aid and CPR is to take a class. If you haven't done so, schedule one as soon as you possibly can. That sort of training is invaluable for everyone but especially for a beginner. There are any number of organizations that teach that sort of material. The Red Cross, American Heart Association and National Safety Council are all organizations from which I have received certification in the basics of first aid. They all teach the same basic "ABCs" of first aid: airway, breathing and circulation. Those are all vital skills you must have and

what I consider the foundation of first aid training. Most of the instructors who teach these courses have extensive training in teaching their organization's particular methodology. However, they oftentimes have little to no real-world experience in actually using most of the skills in their respective programs.

Therefore, I highly recommend you also seek out training from more highly skilled instructors on some of the more advanced topics of wilderness first aid. NOLS Wilderness Medicine Institute, Wilderness Medical Society and any number of private organizations teach more advanced topics. If you seek out a private organization, then find an instructor who has experience using the skills. I have trained with special forces medics, physicians, nurse practitioners, paramedics and emergency medical technicians that run their own organizations. In these types of classes, you may or may not receive a certification. From my perspective, the certification is not as important as having the skills that only an experienced first aid provider can give you. These types of instructors always have numerous accounts they will share in class. This will demonstrate how the skills actually came into play. Most of these instructors are good at teaching how to adapt, improvise and overcome problems that arise.

With all that said, I would like to take the time here to discuss the top four backcountry and remote wilderness issues that come up. In this manner, outside of the training (and whole complete books on the subject that are out there), you can find solutions for these problems. The reason I want to consider these is because I have read of too many stories where simple injuries such as these are the catalysts that started a snowball effect for survival or SAR operations. Since, statistically speaking, these are the most likely, if I can help you prevent and treat them, I will help you avoid allowing them to snowball on you to a worse situation.

KEY CONSIDERATIONS FOR ALL SITUATIONS WHERE FIRST AID MIGHT BE NEEDED

➡ **You are number one. This means that you should not rush into any situation. Be cautious so that you too do not become injured and compound the problem.**

➡ **Do not move patients who have or may have neck or spinal injuries unless certain death is imminent. According to the Wilderness Medicine Institute, 65 percent of all paralysis occurring in outdoor-related events were due to well-meaning people moving an injured person.**

➡ **Talk to the injured person about anything other than the injury while you are assisting them. It will help them keep their mind off of it.**

The top four remote wilderness injuries are:

1. Ankle sprains and breaks (and other lower-extremity issues)

2. Burns

3. Cuts and bleeding

4. Shock

We will look at the preventive measures with each as well as how to handle them in the field.

ANKLE SPRAINS AND BREAKS

The number one injury in a remote wilderness situation is an ankle break or sprain. I will include injuries to the lower extremities as well, since they are often coupled with ankle injuries in the data. Imagine, if you will, that you are on a hike and your hiking partner sprains or breaks their ankle. You will either have to leave them there or assist them in hiking out. In either case, you will want to provide first aid so that the issue is not exacerbated further. If the person stays in the place where the injury occurred, they will deal with the pain more easily if first aid has been applied. If you and the person determine that hiking out is the solution, you will not want the injured area to receive more damage when hopping or limping through the wilderness. Therefore, taking care of this injury is of utmost importance.

PREVENTIVE MEASURES. It may seem simple, but pay attention to where you are going. It is the whole reason I spent the first several chapters of this book detailing how to keep mindful and alert and your thought processes active. Keep your weight centered whenever you need to bound across a rock, log or similar object. This means not extending your foot and leg out unless necessary. When you are in areas that are likely to be slippery, take shorter steps and take your time traversing such an area. Being an adrenaline junkie is going to invite ankle and lower-extremity mechanical injuries. Be more cautious in such activities and if that is not possible, ensure you have the means to fix whatever may arise. Injuries such as these in the backcountry are not only possible but very likely.

Note padding to allow swelling, and sticks to provide rigid support.

TREATMENT. One doctor I trained with expressed that splinting material for an ankle injury should always be "fat and sassy," meaning you should pad the area as much as possible before using a rigid material as a splinting device. Splinting helps to support the injured area so it does not unnecessarily articulate and cause pain or more injury. Splinting material can be trekking poles, sticks, aluminum stays from a pack or basically anything that keeps its shape. Padding can include a blanket, tarp, jacket or vest. Binding material can be any purposed or improvised cordage such as paracord, rope, a belt, a shredded piece of clothing, duct tape, bandanas or vines. In order to splint the ankle, follow these steps:

- ➡ Wrap the ankle in whatever padding material you have.

- ➡ Bind the material once or twice to simply keep it in place.

- ➡ Put the splinting pieces on at least one, but preferably both, sides of the break or strain.

- ➡ Bind it *above* and *below* the injured portion of the ankle or leg.

- ➡ Check to make sure the person can feel their toes and that the area of the injury has room to swell.

BURNS

The number two injury in wilderness situations is burns. These can occur for many reasons, but the two primary ones are inappropriate handling of fire materials and backcountry cooking issues.

PREVENTIVE MEASURES. I build a number of fires each year and one of the things I always make shortly after getting a fire going is a good fire poker. You can do this easily by simply finding a stout woody material that keeps you far enough from the heat of the fire, but short enough that you can effectively move sticks, large wood pieces and coals around in a fire pit. This poker will allow you to keep your distance from the hot materials of the fire that cause injury. In addition, backpacking stoves are most often used to boil water. If you do not pay close attention to them, they boil over and you are then rushing to turn the stove off while boiling water is coming out of it. I recommend you simply get all your dinner preparations made, then start to boil your water. In this manner, you can dedicate your attention to the stove while it is boiling the water. When it first starts to boil, turn it off. If you are using water from an unknown source, it will then be clean. You can then avoid the chance that it starts to boil rapidly and have to turn it off under stress. The second situation that occurs is that people sit on the ground with the stove directly between their legs while cross-legged. The stove can malfunction or water can run over. Both can lead to burns to the inside of the legs and/or genitalia. These are very problematic and painful areas to suffer burns. You should therefore find a stable base to place your stove. Cleared earth, a rock or flat wood are good choices.

TREATMENT. You must consider a burn much like you do any abnormal opening in the body, such as a cut. Burns typically cause severe pain and are very susceptible to infection. Keep in mind that you can have first-, second- and third-degree burns as well. These are the nomenclature medical personnel use to note the severity of the burn. The important thing to remember is that no matter what the severity, treatment is essentially the same:

➡ Wear sterile gloves if possible when working on a burn. It is easy to transfer debris or bacteria from your hands to the wound.

➡ Clear debris from the burn site and expose it to the air. If there is debris that is embedded or stuck in the burn site, leave it. Removing it may cause more damage.

➡ Ensure that you do not touch or make contact with the burn site. If there are blisters, do not pop them or remove them. In other words, do not try to peel off burned skin.

➡ Flush the burned area with clean water.

➡ Cover the area with clean bandages whenever they are available. If you have none, cover it with a clean bandana, article of clothing or even plastic. This will serve to keep from getting more debris in the wound.

➡ Secure the covering. Be advised that utilizing tape on burned skin should be avoided. It is best to tie the bandages. This way, tape glue will not get stuck to skin that is not stable.

➡ If the burn is severe, you will need to monitor and treat shock if it occurs.

CUTS AND BLEEDING

Cuts and the bleeding that result from them are fairly common. Most are simple cuts that will bleed for a short time and then stop. The basics of all cuts is to apply pressure, irrigate the wound site and cover it. I will consider both simple cuts as well as those that are more problematic, such as arterial bleeds.

PREVENTIVE MEASURES. Most cuts in remote situations occur when improperly utilizing sharp tools such as knives and axes. To keep this from happening, never have any part of your body in front of the sharp side of a knife. This often occurs when you are cutting something in one hand with a knife in the other. Take the item that needs to be cut and place it on a log, stump, stick or another hard object that will not dull your knife. When utilizing an ax, maintain your center of balance. Always consider where the ax will travel if it slips on the wood or misses the target. No foot, leg, hand or other person should be near where it might go if it misses its mark. Further, I recommend a particular protocol when in a group setting, especially with children. Whenever a tool (such as a knife, ax or shovel) is about to be used, I require our students to announce, "Tool in the air," and everyone that hears the person say this is then asked to repeat, "Tool in the air." When people follow this protocol, two things occur. One is that the person using the tool will give more attention to what they are doing. Second, those in the area will know that a tool is being used and not walk directly in front of or behind the person using it. This allows the group setting to be safer. Furthermore, when using a cutting tool such as a knife or ax, you should simply go through the motion of where the tool will go if it slips. This way, if something or someone is nearby, you can ask them to move.

Tourniquets should be placed high on the extremity.

TREATMENT FOR SIMPLE CUTS. As I mentioned earlier, there are two distinct types of cuts: those that are simple and bleed a little and those that are more serious and bleed a lot. Those that bleed a lot can be a significant arterial bleed and will be discussed separately from simple cuts. Simple cuts are noted because a minimal amount of blood comes out and it is often described as a simple "draining" from the body. These can occur on nearly any portion of the body. There are only a minimal number of steps to take care of these issues:

→ Hold pressure near the wound to slow the bleeding. Pressure should be applied on the body between the cut and the heart.

→ When bleeding has stopped, irrigate the wound site with clean water. I always carry a syringe in my first aid kit (detailed in Chapter 15). A syringe can be used as a good irrigating device.

→ Cover the cut with a clean bandage. Tape it in such a way that it can be checked regularly for infection.

→ If infection occurs, irrigate with clean water as often as possible and seek medical attention as soon as possible.

TREATMENT FOR SERIOUS CUTS. Serious cuts can be further divided into two subgroups: large open wounds and arterial bleeds. Large open wounds are wounds in which you can see deep tissue, bone or other body portions not normally seen in a small cut. You need to handle these in much the same way as small cuts. Pressure will need to be applied for a much longer period. You will also be well served if you have some rolled gauze, H&H brand bandage or other sterile dressing to pack the large wound site. (Details regarding bandages can be found in Chapter 15.) Arterial bleeds are cuts that have severed or damaged one of the primary arteries that feed blood to your body. They come directly from the heart and they are larger than other arteries. If one of these is cut, you will see blood most often spurting at velocity from the body. It will come out in time with the person's heartbeat. These sorts of bleeds are incredibly serious and need pressure immediately or you risk death of the person in mere minutes. I recommend carrying a tourniquet for this purpose as well. You must have proper training to use one. That is why I have recommended such training for all first aid needs.

MAJOR ARTERIES

Since they are closest to skin level, these three major arteries are more susceptible to being cut:

- ➡ Carotid artery (located along the sides of the neck)
- ➡ Brachial artery (located along the inside of the upper arms)
- ➡ Femoral artery (located along the inside of the upper legs)

SHOCK

Shock is when a person's cardiovascular system cannot or will not provide adequate blood supply to the entire body. This is caused by a range of situations from severe trauma, severe bleeding (internal or external) and even severe allergic reactions.

PREVENTIVE MEASURES. Recognize the warning signs that shock is beginning to occur. Shallow breathing, clammy skin, quick change in pulse rate and loss of consciousness are signs of possible shock. Communicate with the person to get feedback. If feedback is not coming, then address the shock.

TREATMENT. Shock can be treated in the following ways:

- ➡ Lay the person down on dry ground (or use a tarp, packs, leaf litter or similar material if the ground is not dry).

- ➡ Raise their legs—this allows blood to flow from the legs to the organs.

- ➡ Loosen any tight-fitting clothing such as boots, shoes, belts and so on.

- ➡ Cover the person with a sleeping bag, Mylar blanket or any material to help them maintain their usable body heat.

- ➡ Continue to monitor them until their pulse rate stabilizes. Only then should they be moved. If this does not occur, you will need to get help to them.

Treat shock by raising the feet and protecting the person from the ground and air, which rob them of body heat.

SIGNS OF INFECTION

- **Redness**
- **Swelling**
- **White pus**

- **Red streaks**
- **Increase in pain**

OTHER FIRST AID CONSIDERATIONS

While the more common first aid concerns have already been discussed, there are two more concerns that occur less frequently: snakebites and lightning strikes. These do not fall under the auspices of the top four wilderness first aid needs. However, they do cause a fair amount of anxiety for those in the outdoors. I address them here so that you can continue to go outside without as much concern and worry.

SNAKEBITES

Staying away from snakes is the best way to avoid snakebites. The high rate of snakebites to the hand in recent years is a direct result of television edutainment. Handling of snakes is best left to professional biologists.

PREVENTIVE MEASURES. While television may make snake handling look safe or easy, the smartest choice is to just avoid snakes and take these precautions:

- Never pick up a snake. Avoid snakes when possible, and when you must take one for survival food, follow the directions in Chapter 10.

- Avoid walking through tall vegetation. You cannot see what is in front of you. Venomous snakes are rather docile but will strike when they are startled and scared.

- Do not put your hand near any feature (e.g., under rocks, under logs) where you cannot see what is under it. They are great places for snakes to hide—be aware and avoid reaching in or around these areas.

- Study snake behavior in your particular area. Study where they live and seek out food and shelter. Avoid those locations whenever possible.

TREATMENT. The best first aid kit for a venomous snakebite is a set of car keys. There is very little you can do in the wilderness after you have been bitten. You need medical attention as soon as possible. There are a number of snakebite kits that are sold in outdoor outlets. Avoid these devices. Due to the organic nature of snake venom, it attaches itself to muscle or blood at the molecular level. Therefore, it cannot be "sucked out" by these devices or the human mouth. That only serves to give false security to the person that has been bitten. Beyond those thoughts, here are some other options for treating a snakebite:

- Wash the bite sight to help avoid infection.

- Keep the person calm.

- Remove all restrictive clothing and jewelry.

- If you are less than 30 minutes from a vehicle, bring the vehicle to the person if possible. If a vehicle is farther away, the person is going to need to get out of the wilderness and seek medical attention immediately.

- The latest information available at the time of this writing was to not bandage or otherwise restrict the flow of venom in the body. To do so leaves it concentrated in one location and will therefore make that portion of the body more susceptible to loss due to swelling.

LIGHTNING STRIKES

Spend enough time outside and you will certainly be caught out in a storm. Lightning is a real threat and should be avoided at all costs. These are three items of consideration to avoid lightning:

1. Pay attention to the weather and start seeking appropriate shelter whenever possible.

2. Avoid open areas and objects that are taller than everything else in the vicinity. Get off hilltops and away from the tallest trees.

3. Stay away from objects that conduct electricity (e.g., cell towers, power lines, tent poles, trekking poles).

LAND NAVIGATION

I spend a great deal of time and effort focusing on preventive measures to keep you safe. It is my goal to always help you spend more time in the wilderness rather than less. That can be done in such a way that you are safer while you are there. There is no better skill set to help keep you safe than land navigation. *Land navigation* is a term I am borrowing from the military. You may have heard the process by its full name or by parts of it. *Orienteering*, *map and compass skills*, *reading a map*, *taking a bearing* and *shooting an azimuth* are all phrases that are used when one considers going into an unknown area and being able to return safely. The key to understanding these kills is to understand each of the different parts and then how to use them together. Let's first take a look at four different sets of maps.

Maps are nothing more than a representation, sometimes even a picture, of Earth's surface. Some maps are much more accurate than others. With more accuracy also comes confusion for those with an untrained eye. Let us first make sure you can recognize the difference in maps that you will often have access to.

LOCAL MAPS are typically put together by someone local, who oftentimes does not have good drawing or computer skills. They will be drawn by memory and will often have man-made features added in for reference, such as signs, buildings and so on. These are notorious for not being drawn to scale. This means that they do not accurately represent distances well. It is rare that they will show any changes in elevation, streams and creeks or other land-based features. You will often find these at parks, nature preserves and small wilderness areas. They provide the user with just enough information to get out of the vehicle, find a trail or other feature, hike a bit and head back home.

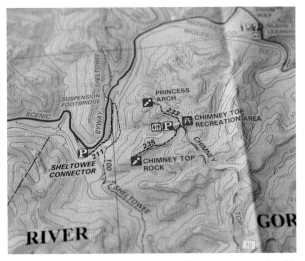

Topography maps are must-have items with large amounts of useful information on them.

SCALE 1:24 000

1 unit on the map = 24,000 units on Earth.

TRAIL MAPS are maps that are more professionally put together. They will often list more land features, such as open areas versus forested ones, trails, streams, landmarks of interest, roads and more. Trail maps are generally distributed by some government entity that has staff that can invest a fair amount of time into the graphic representation of the area. Day hikers, backpackers and those who want to stick to a trail system will find these incredibly useful as long as they are available for the area you want to visit. They are most often drawn to scale and indicate north correctly. They also fold up and store nicely.

TOPOGRAPHY MAPS are most often referred to as topo maps or quads. For accuracy, these are the best maps you can get for both on- and off-trail travel. They are incredibly accurate and are full of details. Topo maps of nearly the entire world are available to everyone through the Internet. The U.S. federal government oversees the United States Geological Survey (USGS), which is responsible for these topo maps.

MAPPING SOFTWARE includes any number of mapping software and websites available to us. Some of these will come at a cost, others will come for free. I have listed this as a separate style of map simply because of the customization it allows the user. With this customization, you can add way points of locations and note distances very easily as well as add or take away various layers of topography or similar data. You as the user need to ensure you know how to use the settings correctly when utilizing mapping software and particularly when printing the maps. You do not want to assume you have printed a map that indicates true north when it actually represents magnetic north or vice versa. When printing maps, you want to ensure the printing function does not change the actual size as it relates to your scale. If you have a scale that represents 1:24000, where the *1* represents 1 inch (3 cm), then verify that the scale that is printed is actually 1 inch (3 cm).

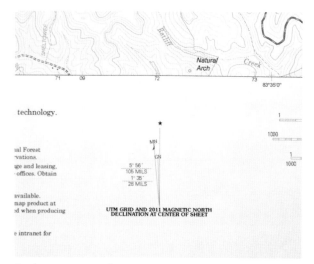

Quality topo maps will give you the declination of the area you are traveling.

Topography maps are the most useful and what I recommend people utilize, but they can be confusing to a new user. Let's take a closer look at them, so you can be sure of the information found on them:

- ➡ *Scale* is typically found in the lower right corner of a topography map. You will recognize it with a number that looks like the following: *1:24000*. This is a ratio that 1 unit of distance on the map is equal to 24,000 units of that distance on the actual Earth. For example, if you measure the distance between two ridges on a topography map and find the distance to be 1 inch (3 cm), the actual distance on Earth is 24,000 inches (2,000 feet, or roughly ⅓ of a mile [610 m, or 0.6 km]).

- ➡ Topography maps include a *north indicator*. There are many angles of measurement that can be accurately referred to as north. When you lay a map in front of you and the writing on it is right-side up, then the top of the map is going to be north. This does not give you the accuracy that you need to adequately navigate using the map.

That is why good topography maps will have the north indicator arrows on the bottom. You will notice that there are three "norths" in this regard (see page 57).

- ➡ This difference between true north and magnetic north is referred to as *declination*. It varies widely across the planet, and you must know what this variance is for the portion of the world you want to trek into. For example, the declination on the East coast in Maine is 20 degrees west and is approximately 18 degrees east for most of California. This topic is hard for many to understand. I have had some good teachers to assist me along the way and have also come up with my unique ways of communicating this variance to my students. One way of remembering the declination is by remembering that "west is best; east is least." This is a simple way of explaining that you add degrees of measurement when you have a westerly declination and you subtract degrees of measurement when you have an easterly declination. An example can be found here in our area. The declination is 6 degrees west. This means if I determine an angle of measure on my map to be 240 degrees (which is based upon true north), then the setting on my compass should be 246 degrees (magnetic north).

- ➡ The *grid system* is incredibly important when ensuring that when you are working, training or otherwise communicating with others, you are "speaking the same language." All maps will have a grid system that helps to set coordinates for the map itself. Refer to page 57 to see the most common ones.

THE THREE "NORTHS"

TRUE NORTH: This is the geographic direction that is represented by lines of longitude on a map. These lines begin and end at Earth's poles.

MAGNETIC NORTH: The north pole is in a constant state of movement. This causes the north arrow on your compass to vary slightly from the true north. This difference between true north and magnetic north is referred to as declination.

GRID NORTH: This is the direction that your map grid system lines will indicate.

GRID SYSTEMS

MILITARY GRID REFERENCE SYSTEM (MGRS): This is used primarily by the U.S. military and the same system is used throughout all branches of the military.

UNIVERSAL TRANSVERSE MERCATOR (UTM): This is a common grid system still in great use by many SAR teams.

UNITED STATES NATIONAL GRID SYSTEM (USNG): This is the system that most professional organizations are going to. The newest USGS quad maps include the USNG tick marks and grid reference numbers.

LAT AND LONG: This system is used by many commercial pilots of rotary and fixed-wing aircraft as well as many organizations dependent upon outdated maps and equipment. It's the same system schoolchildren are still taught, because it is not based on the metric system and the others are.

COLORS ON A TOPO MAP

BLACK: Man-made objects

BROWN: Contour lines

BLUE: Water

GREEN: Forested areas

WHITE: Open areas

RED: Trails

COMPASSES

Compasses are some of the oldest "modern" technology that we have. When choosing a compass for land-navigation purposes, there are a few things that are imperative to understand:

- It should be a liquid-filled compass. Those without a liquid-filled housing are subpar and often indicate incorrect direction.

- You should choose one that does not have bubbles in the housing. Bubbles in the liquid will also often provide an incorrect reading.

- Choose one that you feel you can train with. Training with a compass is key and if it is confusing to you, you will not train with it regularly. There are two main choices that I will detail shortly.

- Make sure that the bezel on a baseplate compass does not move on the housing other than spin around it. If it moves side to side, choose another one.

There are two main types of compasses that are useful to our needs: baseplate compasses and lensatic compasses. These photos and descriptions will help you understand how to use them. Let us take a look at them individually first and then how to use them.

BASEPLATE COMPASSES

BEZEL: This is the rotating portion of the compass which indicates 0 to 360 degrees of measurement, most often in 2-degree increments noted by each tick mark. The four cardinal directions (north, south, east and west) are indicated by their corresponding first letter.

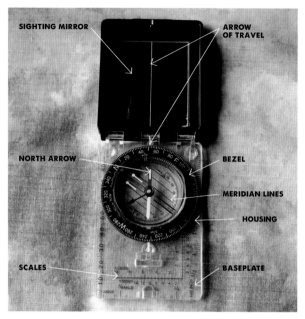

Understanding the importance of each part of the compass you choose is critical.

BASEPLATE: The base of the compass will have various scales depending upon the model you choose. Some models have scales that correspond directly to a USGS topo map of 1:24000 design. They will also often include English standard and metric measurement scales or rulers on them as well.

ARROW OF TRAVEL: This is the stationary arrow on the compass that should always point in the direction you want to go.

NORTH ARROW: This is the arrow within the liquid-filled housing that rotates. Models vary but on most compasses, the red arrow points north.

MERIDIAN LINES: These are the lines within the bezel that rotate when you turn it. These lines will correspond directly to the map grid lines.

SIGHTING MIRROR/COVER: This is an optional piece to baseplate compasses that allows you to more accurately determine your bearing. The mirror allows you to look down on the compass itself while you are holding the compass in cheek hold— in other words, placing the baseplate to your cheek to take a more accurate reading.

OTHER ITEMS: There are many different "bells and whistles" that will come along with the various models out there. However, the ones listed here are the standard ones needed to use a baseplate compass adequately.

LENSATIC COMPASSES

BEZEL: This is the rotating ring.

ARROW: Luminous and magnetic, the arrow on a lensatic compass clearly points north.

FLOATING DIAL: This is the portion containing the degrees of measurement.

THUMB LOOP: This is the portion you slip your thumb through when taking an azimuth.

FRONT SIGHT: This is the slot closest to your face when you use the compass. It also contains a lens by which you can clearly see the floating dial.

BACK SIGHT: This is a wire on the compass across from your face that you line up with the spot you are taking an azimuth on.

STRAIGHT EDGE: This is the side of the compass with graduated markings for scale.

UTILIZING THE MAP AND COMPASS TOGETHER

Studying the use of maps and compasses should be an ever-present part of your outdoor training. Each time I work with military units, I find that land navigation is one of those skills they are always up to speed with. It is dependent upon the unit, but nearly all military units that would need these skills regularly engage in this training. Take that as a sign that you should be doing the same. I mention this because there are any number of resources that dig into the intricacies of land navigation with a map and compass. In this text, I want to show you the six simple steps that will help you determine an azimuth. For these points I will utilize a baseplate compass.

1. Identify your position and the area you want to travel to on the map. You can then connect the two points with your pencil or with an imaginary line.

2. Place the edge of your compass on the line.

(continued)

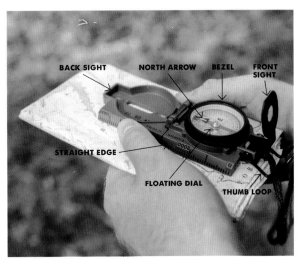

Line your compass up with the boundary or grid lines of your map.

3. Rotate the bezel so that the lines inside the compass (meridian lines) are parallel or directly on the map's lines pointing to true north. This can be done with the edge of the map as well. If you look at your compass, you will notice that there is a degree measurement in line with the direction-of-travel arrow.

4. Adjust your compass for declination.

5. To start walking in the appropriate direction, hold the compass in either center hold or cheek hold and rotate your body until the magnetic north arrow lines up with the orienting arrow of the compass.

6. If you look directly along the imaginary line that leads from the direction-of-travel arrow, you will then be going in the appropriate direction.

Each bead on the bottom represents 100 meters (328 ft). When they are all pulled, you then utilize a bead on top that represents a kilometer (0.6 mi).

PACE COUNT

Pace count is another one of those skills that serves very well as a preventive to a survival situation, but you must develop it before you need it. Your pace count is the number of paces that you take to travel a known distance. Typically, this distance is 328 feet (100 m). Designate a travel corridor that is flat and easy to walk. Walk the 328-foot (100-m) distance and count every time your left foot hits the ground. In this manner, you will then note that for every certain number of steps, you have walked 328 feet (100 m). As an example, my pace count is 68. Therefore, every time I place my left foot, I count. And once I hit 68, I know I am approximately at 328 feet (100 m) into the walk. If you want to become incredibly technical with this, you can follow the example of any good infantryman (especially the Rangers or Marines). Most of them will know their pace count walking on flat ground, uphill, downhill, with a pack, without a pack and so on. In this manner, they are prepared to know their distance into an area just by counting steps. Pace count beads (a.k.a. Ranger beads) are a way to help you keep track of the steps. You can pull a bead each time you hit 328 feet (100 m). Once you reach 10, you know you have walked 3,280 feet (1 km) into your trek. You can also do this with rocks or other small items in your pocket. Every time you walk 328 feet (100 m), move one of ten rocks from your left pocket to the right. Once your pocket is empty you know you have walked 3,280 feet (1 km).

DEAD RECKONING

Dead reckoning is the practice of determining one's location based upon a known fixed point. In dead reckoning (sometimes spelled *ded reckoning*, for *deduced reckoning*) you approximate your position on a map from that known fixed point based upon your pace count and estimated time to travel that distance. You have starting point A and you know from your pace count that you have walked approximately 984 feet (300 m). You can then look at your map and note where you have traveled. This is more accurately done if those lines of travel are nearly straight.

PUT IT INTO PRACTICE

➡ First, get a topography map of the outdoor area that you like to visit. Study it and make sure you can read and locate the features I have listed for regarding maps (e.g., scale, colors, declination).

➡ Determine a long topographical feature such as a river, road or straight section of a trail. I would recommend for starters that you keep this distance around the 328-feet (100-m) mark.

➡ Find a good starting point for yourself on the map. This will most likely be a spot for you to park your vehicle that is legal and safe.

➡ Determine, by utilizing your scale, what the distance is from your parking spot to an area along the topographical feature. Bonus points for using dead reckoning along the feature and then traveling to what you are looking for. Once you determine how far it is, use your pace count you determined earlier to calculate how many steps you are going to take to get there.

➡ Once you decide where you want to travel, then determine the bearing from the parking spot to your destination.

➡ On a piece of paper, write down what kind of topographical features you will cover while going to your destination. Examples could include going over a stream, next to a cliff and so on.

➡ Now drive to your parking spot. Review your notes. Take your bearing (after adjusting for declination) and away you go. Keep up with your pace count as you go so you know how far you have walked.

➡ Once you find your destination, you should be able to easily take a reverse bearing and make your way back to your vehicle.

➡ The key to this (and all the other skills) is to revise and repeat. Some of the skills practices may not go as planned. Continue to practice; do not give up. You can then repeat the skills until they become more ingrained. With land navigation, this simply means to determine another destination and travel to and from it.

SELF-DEFENSE

Like many topics in this book, self-defense can be broken down into infinite details and comprise its own book. The subject, at its core, is more simple than that. You do need to understand it from the mind-set, skills, techniques and gear perspective.

Self-defense mind-set focuses on your ability to master the "Double A," as I like to call it: avoidance and awareness. If you can avoid confrontations, whether with other humans or wildlife, you do not have the need to engage them physically. Assault from other humans comes in two forms: ego-based assault and predator-based assault. If you can keep your ego in check, you will avoid most ego-based situations. If you are aware of what is going on around you (refer to Chapters 1–5), you will avoid most predator-based assaults. Solutions for wildlife-based assaults are fairly simple. Do what you can to avoid their young and their food source. These are the two driving forces for wildlife, and if you can focus your attention on those strategies, you can keep yourself out of harm's way.

Let's assume you have found yourself in a situation where the avoidance and awareness strategy has not worked for a human you have made contact with. Please note that all humans have five weapons on them at all times. In relation to that, all humans also have five vulnerable areas of the body. At its core, your self-defense involves using one of your weapons to strike one of your aggressor's five vulnerable ones.

If an aggressor comes within reach of you, it will be necessary to strike them with speed and a high rate of violence of action (the use of surprise, strength, speed and aggressiveness to achieve dominance over an aggressor). Assault such as this causes an anaerobic reaction in the body, meaning that your heart rate and breathing rise and fall quickly. Unless you train in this manner regularly, this will cause an oxygen deficiency in the bloodstream, which leads to muscle weakness. This is why you need to attack with all you have until the threat is neutralized, meaning you can either get away to safety or you are no longer being assaulted by the threat. For example, if someone grabs you and pins your arms, use your knees and feet to attack the groin. If someone throws you to the ground and grabs your feet, use your hands and elbows. The mind-set that is important to remember is to not allow yourself to be a victim. You must fight with all you have until you can no longer fight.

FIVE WEAPONS

- Head
- Hands
- Elbows
- Knees
- Feet

FIVE VULNERABLE AREAS

- Face (particularly eyes and nose)
- Throat
- Groin
- Knees
- Feet

Unbalance with a strike first, then sweep the nearby leg out from your agressor.

Unbalance with a strike first, then grab the head and throw over your hip, the body will follow.

Your goal should always be to keep someone outside of striking distance. This is the reason I react so quickly when someone comes into my reach. I want you to be able to defend yourself when an aggressor is grabbing or pinning you or otherwise in close body-to-body contact with you. There are two maneuvers to keep in mind when this occurs: throwing the head and sweeping the leg (see sidebar below).

I highly recommend that you visit a facility where you can see the martial arts of Krav Maga or judo in action. Other arts are often incredibly technical. They are worthwhile endeavors for certain; however, the technical details will often get a new person bogged down. Both Krav Maga and judo spend a great deal of time considering the two methods mentioned here. Please be advised that you will see very refined and detailed movements being practiced. If you desire to practice, they will most assuredly allow you to join them. If you do not, it will be easy enough to watch a class or two and get a good idea how to use some of these methods for self-defense. There are any number of videos on YouTube where you can see this sort of practice as well.

BASICS OF GRAPPLING

THROW THE HEAD; the body will follow.

SWEEP AND/OR KICK A LEG OUT; the body will follow.

Another very important consideration is what to do if you go to the ground. If you spend much time discussing this topic with others, whether they are trained or not, you will almost always hear someone say, "All fights end up on the ground," meaning the person being assaulted and the person assaulting them purposely or inadvertently both go to the ground. This is absolutely not true. Most fights between *untrained* individuals go to the ground. You need to train and do all you can to not go to the ground.

If you do end up there, you need to keep a few things in mind to protect yourself until you can get back to your feet:

➡ Get to your back and fight with your five weapons. You cannot do this if you are face-down.

➡ "Keep your elbows to your knees and your knees to your elbows," is a common thing I say in grappling. Think of it as being in the fetal position on your back. This offers you the ability to use your arms to cover your head, and your legs to cover your abdomen. Both of these areas of the body are vulnerable in any attack and protecting them is important.

➡ Create distance and get back to your feet. This might mean striking to get away then getting back up, but you must get back to your feet as soon as possible.

➡ Another great option is to bite your aggressor. There are a number of assaults that have ended with the victim biting off an ear, nose or other section of the body to get the aggressor off them. The pain is so intense it is difficult for the aggressor to continue at that time, which is often enough time for you to get away.

ARMED DEFENSE

Weapons of self-defense are tools, and like any other tool, you must learn how to use them properly to defend yourself. Weapons of opportunity (such as a stout stick, rock or similar item) are effective for arming yourself in the wilderness. Just bear in mind that bringing harm to other humans is a situation where there will be emotional and possibly legal ramifications to deal with. Virtually no one wants to bring that harm to someone else, but in the case of someone assaulting you, defending yourself is something you must consider now before it occurs. Armed defense is a way that you can defend yourself at a farther distance. The closer an aggressor comes to you, the higher the possibility for them to bring harm to you. If you can keep them at a distance with a knife, pepper spray or gun, you have the ability to protect yourself without coming into contact with them.

Let's consider the four most common self-defense tools and pros and cons of each.

(Note: Necessary safety precautions were taken to ensure firearms were safe during the training in these photos.)

PEPPER SPRAY AND MACE

These sprays come in varying degrees of intensity. Pepper spray is also called oleoresin capsicum and is concentrated pepper particles. Mace is a chemical irritant. They both serve the same purpose, which is to cause irritation to the eyes, throat and lungs when ingested. This irritant will cause varying degrees of watering of the eyes, phlegm loosening and more in individuals that have extreme issue with it. There are also versions of this made into bear spray, to help thwart a bear attack. However, the effect is not instantaneous. This means that if you spray a bear or person, you will still need to remove yourself from the situation. Seconds later, the effects will start and it is difficult for the aggressor to function.

Know how to use your weapon to both shoot and to strike an aggressor.

A stick weighted on one end allows you to use physics to defend yourself.

A knife used with a firm grip and in concert with good defensive skills is a force multiplier.

BATONS AND STICKS

These can be as technical as a collapsible baton most often associated with law enforcement and as simple as a stick. These weapons are used to cause blunt-force trauma to another individual and are nearly useless on a wild animal. Targets are the same vulnerable areas mentioned previously; however, you can add in an attack to the hands and arms as well. This serves to keep an aggressor from being able to grab you.

KNIVES

Knives are actually one of the most-carried items for self-defense—but they are the least effective. Not because they are not a useful tool, but because people do not train with them often enough (sometimes never). I have had dozens of students come to self-defense seminars and say they carry a knife and have never trained with it. You must train with this weapon to use it effectively and ensure you do not injure yourself at the same time. Technical proficiency is vital to the use of a knife. Also, some aggressors are wary of attacking someone wielding a knife, so simply being ready to defend yourself with one is beneficial. The simplest method (if you do not have time or desire to regularly train) is to slash in an *X* pattern in front of you. This pattern makes it more difficult for an aggressor to move close to you while also defending themselves. The angles of an *X* are more difficult to deal with than those of a lowercase *t*.

JEFF COOPER'S FOUR RULES OF GUN SAFETY

1. Treat all guns as if they are loaded.

2. Never point a gun at anything you are not willing to destroy.

3. Keep your finger off the trigger until your sights are on the target and you have made the decision to shoot.

4. Be sure of your target and what lies beyond it.

GUNS

A gun is a force equalizer, that is for certain. This means that it can easily make a person that is small or incapable of defense against a larger aggressor immediately able to take care of themselves. Guns are certainly one of those items you *must* train with regularly to be proficient in. Even getting your hands on the weapon—whether it be on your belt, in your pocket or in your purse—is vital to practice. Always keep in mind the four rules of gun safety when utilizing one in training, carrying it for peace of mind or using it to defend yourself.

The late Lt. Col. Jeff Cooper, a World War II and Korean War veteran and founder of Gunsite Academy, was an incredible shooting instructor with a wonderful ability to break down complex processes into teaching points easy for everyone to understand. Please see the sidebar above for his four rules of gun safety. More importantly, make them part of any activity in which weapons are used.

A handgun is easy to conceal when legal to do so.

CHAPTER 7

MAINTAINING YOUR CORE BODY TEMPERATURE THROUGH CLOTHING AND SHELTER

AT NIGHT MAKE ME ONE WITH THE DARKNESS; IN THE MORNING MAKE ME ONE WITH THE LIGHT.

—WENDELL BERRY

In December 2015, two hunting buddies and their hunting dog set out to go duck hunting in Oklahoma. They were out in the middle of an intense cold-weather storm. Wind speed was 45 mph (72 kph) and the wind chill temperature was 15°F (-9°C). Upon leaving, one of the hunters even tweeted an ominous message saying he was going out in a bad storm to hunt ducks in case no one heard from them.

What exactly happened to them will most likely never be known. After they did not return home in a timely fashion, authorities were notified and searched the area. They found the hunters' capsized boat and much of the gear near the shore. One of the men was also found dead near the boat. After another week they found the body of the other man several yards into the shoreline among some thick brush. Both men had died of hypothermia. The dog was found alive.

Much can be done in a situation like this to keep it from becoming a tragedy. I am an advocate of pushing oneself to the limits in bad conditions. It is how most highly trained outdoorsmen become stronger and more skilled. The key to doing this is to take the necessary precautions to be there. Those precautions would include the following:

- Understand the difference between confidence and cockiness. The tweets indicated they were cocky and ignoring the obvious anomalies of an average situation. As I discussed in Section 1, ignoring the anomalies is one of the first steps toward possible disaster.

- Let others know where you are going and when you're expecting to return. These two people were focused on themselves and no one else. That is fine if they have their own plan for self-rescue, which, in this case, they did not.

- Remain humble. Also in Section 1, I addressed the need to continually self-assess. If these two gentlemen had assessed themselves and stacked that up to the situation and remained humble, they would have recognized that this was adding up to a bad situation, not a good one.

- Hope for the best, plan for the worst. They did just the opposite and it cost them their lives.

Here is a listing of the simple gear pieces these men could have had that would have saved their lives that day:

LIFE VESTS: They were not wearing them.

SIGNAL CLOTHING: Both men were wearing camouflage, which made it difficult to find the second man who had crawled into the brush.

BEACON: Some models will start when they make contact with water, others must be turned on manually.

WATERPROOF CELL PHONE CONTAINERS: The men were within range for service, but both phones had become inoperable due to being soaked in the water.

EXTRA CLOTHING: They had good clothes on for cold weather; they did not have good clothes on if they got wet.

Here is how this situation could have gone if these items would have been in place:

The boat is capsized and the hunters, with life vests on, swim to shore without burning too many calories in the process. They employ their emergency beacons. They remove their cell phones from the protective cases and phone authorities. They remove their wet clothing and put on a change of clothing *or* they stay in the clothing they have on, which happens to be wool or fleece that insulates when it is wet.

TAKE IT ONE STEP FURTHER

If they simply had a ferrocerium rod and fire-starting cubes in their life vests, they could have started a fire while they waited for rescue. If that was not available, and since they both made it out of the water due to their life vests, they could have conserved body heat by laying together along with the dog, utilizing one another's body heat for warmth.

The top reason for death in a wilderness setting is due to exposure. Read that again: the top reason for death in a wilderness situation is exposure. Exposure is the technical way of saying the elements were harsh enough to a person that they succumbed to them. Going further, hypothermia is the loss of core body temperature and hyperthermia is a rise in core body temperature. The vast majority of these deaths are due to hypothermia. The reason I want you to pay close attention is simple.

If everyone who reads this book follows these methods in their wilderness adventures, it will most likely stop needless deaths. I want to focus on maintaining your core body temperature from five different perspectives:

1. Understanding heat principles and their importance

2. Understanding that clothing choices can make or break you

3. Utilizing natural materials to develop shelter

4. Setting up a bombproof tarp

5. Getting comfortable without carrying too much weight

UNDERSTANDING HEAT PRINCIPLES AND THEIR IMPORTANCE

I am going to focus most of our discussion here on a situation where you must not get too cold. Getting too hot is not as likely, so I will therefore give thought on it briefly at the end of each section.

You must first understand that our bodies are the only "heaters" that are realistically going to be carried into a wilderness setting with us. You must therefore set it up for success rather than failure. Thermoregulation is the process that your body goes through to regulate its temperature despite what outside influences are put on it. More specifically, homeostasis is the process that occurs within our body to effect body temperature.

This system is mostly reactionary, meaning that when your body starts to detect that the outside temperature is changing, only then can it start the enzyme process that will assist it in warming up. There is a limit to how much it can warm up due to these outside influences. You will note that your body will increase its temperature

in response to inside influences in a more dramatic manner. This is a fever. This is simply the body's defense mechanism against infection or other influences inside of the body.

What the body does do remarkably well is prioritize portions of itself as being areas that are more sensitive to thermoregulation and must have heat. It recognizes that at times it must sacrifice certain portions of itself to maintain the others. This is why when you start to get cold the first things that typically get cold are your hands and feet. Your body is recognizing that you are getting cold. It knows that your organs are vital to your living but, as an example, it can lose a finger and still survive. Therefore, when your body recognizes it is getting cold, it will decrease the blood flow to your extremities and use it in the core of your body.

One of the simplest techniques I know to assist you in this I learned from a special forces operator during a trip that I was guiding. He showed me that simply rubbing your core will help trick your organs into "thinking" that they are warm. In so doing your body will release some of the blood in the core of your body to your extremities. It is a simple technique, but it works. This technique is one of several methods of heat transfer.

Heat transfer is the simple exchange of heat from your body to and from the environment.

UNDERSTANDING THAT CLOTHING CHOICES CAN MAKE OR BREAK YOU

With that understanding, you can now get dressed for success. Someone, somewhere has told you to dress in layers. Whoever that was, they were right. The key to you remaining at the correct temperature is to wear the right clothes. I am going to break this down from the base layer on up.

FOUR METHODS OF HEAT TRANSFER

1. **Radiation** is where electromagnetic heat waves radiate from a source. Examples of a source are the sun, a fire, hand warmer or fuel heater.

2. **Evaporation** is when a person sweats or is otherwise wet and heat is removed from the body through heat transfer into the water droplets. Your body heats up the sweat or water molecules, which in turn evaporate and leave.

3. **Convection** is the process of exchange of heat temperatures through a liquid or gas. This means heat leaves a surface (your body) and is then captured in an area that is cooler (e.g., your jacket or sleeping bag). This is a circular pattern where this exchange continues to occur.

4. **Conduction** is when heat is exchanged when two surfaces come into direct contact with each another. An example would be you lying down on the ground. The heat from your body will be conducted into the earth.

THE BASE LAYER rests against your skin. In cold weather, this must be something that is going to wick moisture away from your skin. The old adage of "cotton kills" is so very true. Cotton holds moisture against your skin. Evaporation occurs, and therefore you are cooled off. Some good choices for base layers are:

➡ **POLYPROPYLENE:** This is a synthetic material that has been used extensively by the U.S. military as a base layer for many years.

➡ **WOOL:** Wool has come a long way in the last few years. For many, wool is an itchy, uncomfortable fabric. Modern processing has taken merino, alpaca and other wool types to a whole new level of warmth and comfort.

➡ **POLYESTER:** I am not talking about your grandad's leisure suit here. I am referring to the various products made inexpensively that wick moisture away from your skin. Most base-layer producers utilize some variation of polyester in their materials.

THE SECONDARY LAYER goes on the base layer. The outside influences will dictate the materials made here. Whenever possible, I like to have a sturdy pair of pants that have some variation of water repellent on them. Even if no rain is present, just keeping the morning dew off of me is important for survival. My above-the-waist secondary layer should be another garment that is wicking. I typically wear a polar fleece shirt, jacket and/or vest on this layer.

THE TERTIARY LAYER is what I would consider the final layer and is completely dependent upon the environment you will be involved in. There are certainly some basics that I recommend. A two-part jacket system is ideal. The inner layer should ideally be an insulator. Synthetic material such as polyester fiberfill is a great insulator, as is down. Just bear in mind that if you are regularly in wet weather or near water and the down gets wet, it no longer insulates. The outermost layer needs to be water- and wind-proof. For the reasons of heat transfer above, you must have this for your outer layer. If you get wet, or the wind removes the heat from you, your core body temp will lower.

THERE ARE SOME EXTRAS that I highly recommend you have with you as well:

- A hat needs to be of wicking material. It needs to be one that you can easily take off and put on to help regulate your temperature and not easily lose it.

- Gloves are also helpful. Remember the principle of heat conduction discussed earlier? That is why I like to have mittens that can fold back to expose my fingers. In this manner I can do the work needed with my fingers but when no work is being done, I can cover my fingers and allow them to rest alongside one another. This allows conduction to occur between fingers.

- A scarf or keffiyeh (also called a shemagh) is something that you can wrap around your neck and face if the need arises.

I have mentioned regulating your temperature more than once. I will detail that for you as well. I have a rule of thumb for this. Whenever I am doing work such that my body temperature will naturally rise (e.g., setting up shelter, gathering fire materials), I will unbutton or unzip near my chest, take off my scarf and remove my hat. As soon as I get any sense of a "chill," I will reverse that one by one. For example, as soon as I feel that chill come on, I might simply replace my hat. If it continues, I will button up and so on.

The reason I do this is simple. It is natural for your body to warm up with movement, and if you capture all of that heat by being buttoned up, you can easily overheat. When you overheat, you sweat; when you sweat and then stop activity, you will more easily cool your core body down. This is what I do not want to happen.

UTILIZING NATURAL MATERIALS TO DEVELOP SHELTER

Debris huts are the shelters that most survival schools across the country will show you how to build. Also pick up any other book and they will detail the construction of them. Let me be clear that I am not a fan of them at all. Let me point out how these things are typically taught:

- Gather everyone in a class and teach them how to build it.

- Have the class build the structure, sometimes using rakes and tarps to gather materials.

- Build a nice little cave of branches and leaves.

- Use it as a nice photo opportunity.

I am detailing this because this book is full of things you should do as well as things you should avoid doing.

Building a debris hut is one to avoid and here is why:

- A debris hut is typically only big enough for one person.

- It will take 10–20 people about one hour to build an adequate shelter. That is 10–20 man hours. This means a solo person building one for themselves will need 10–20 hours to build it.

- To do that means you will burn an incredible amount of energy and water and set yourself up to be colder due to sweat.

- Laying down on the ground in a debris hut is a disaster waiting to happen. As I have already discussed, the earth serves as a conductor to body heat. If you build the Taj Mahal of debris huts and lay down on the ground inside of it, it will not prevent your body heat from entering the ground. Although many debris huts are filled with leaves, it is difficult at best to crawl into one and keep plenty of leaves between you and the ground. You will still get cold.

Now that I have debunked one of the worst methods, let's take a look at two simple structures that can be built from natural materials. One is what I call a squirrel's nest. The other is the open-faced lean-to.

SQUIRREL'S NEST

A squirrel's nest is very simple and quick to put together. It will require you to pile up as many leaves as possible. An adequate amount is head high. Put a few branches on top to hold the pile together and then slide into the middle of the pile of leaves. It is not ideal, but it is simpler, uses less caloric expenditure and is the same method that squirrels actually use for nests in nesting cavities and tree tops. When entering the nest, just ensure there are plenty of leaves between you and the ground to keep you from having the heat of your body conducted away. The key to this is its placement. If you can find an overturned tree with a large root ball exposed, build next to it. Better still would be between a hill and rock or similar natural feature, so that you can keep as many leaves together as you can and ward off any winds that will most likely pass through. Wind serves to pull heat away from the nest (remember, your body is the only heater you have). One problem with this structure is that it is a short-term solution. You will also have leaves surrounding you, on your face and so on.

OPEN-FACED LEAN-TO

Lean-tos come in many shapes and sizes. At their core they have a ridgeline, a slanted wall that is toward the prevailing winds and an open face on one side as well as a few small logs, rocks or similar items to form a border on the open face. The border portions will serve to hold leaves in place so you can form a bed. This structure works very well in tandem with a fire on the face side of the structure. Heat is radiated from the fire to the shelter where it is somewhat retained. With any structure, take advantage of the natural landscape to build as much of it for you as you can. This means if you have a stable downed tree, then use either the tree trunk or the upturned root ball as the basis for the structure.

In this manner, you do not have to spend as much energy and time building it. You let nature do some of it for you. The downfall to this structure is that it can allow a fair amount of moisture and rain in through the face of it if not properly built.

Those are two very simple and easy-to-build structures for anyone—even someone who is injured can scrape up enough leaves to make a squirrel's nest. Keep in mind for both of those that if your intent is to stay in them until help arrives, you will need to do something to bring attention to its position. If you have any type of brightly colored clothing, then tear a piece of it off and tie it to the top of the structure or tie it over a branch near the structure. If that is not available, change up the vegetation that surrounds it. Disturbance is what trackers refer to as anything that differs from base line. A well-trained SAR tracker should see leaves that are overturned, branches that are broken, grasses that are twisted and much more. I point this out because if you are making a shelter from natural materials it will look like the surrounding material and blend in, in essence making it camouflaged. You do not want this to be the case in a situation where you want to be found.

When there is no gear available, use your surroundings to build shelter.

SETTING UP A BOMBPROOF TARP

I am a big advocate of utilizing tarps for several reasons, but primarily because they are multiuse and they save you loads of time and effort when utilizing them to build a shelter. Not all tarps are created equal. I recommend tarps that have the following attributes:

NYLON: It resists acids, UV rays and alkalines and is still reasonably light.

RIPSTOP: One tear will not ruin the tarp and it makes it strong enough to carry people, firewood or rocks if there is need to do so.

GROMMETS: Take a good look at the tarp you are considering and ensure the grommets are placed well. Do not use one with cloth loops; they break down more easily.

SIZE: If you are going to get a tarp, get one that is bigger than just for individual use (approximately 9 x 9 feet [274 x 274 cm]). Military ponchos (4 x 5 feet [122 x 152 cm]) are incredible pieces of equipment for one person but not big enough for multiple people.

KNOTS FOR TARP SETUP

HALF-HITCH: Used to secure one or both sides of a ridgeline. Usually setup with two half-hitches to make it more secure.

TRUCKER'S HITCH (A.K.A. CANOE MAN'S HITCH): The standard bearer for setting up a pulley system to increase tension on the ridgeline.

TAUT LINE HITCH: A knot that slides so that a stake can be used to increase or lessen tension based upon the setup's needs.

PRUSIK: Another knot that will slide along another rope but will secure when tension is placed on it. Prusiks are best used when the rope you are tying to is larger in diameter than the one you make the Prusik.

Setting up a tarp is simple, especially when you understand the fundamentals of any setup you want to try:

- Prevailing winds need to hit a side that is staked to the ground, not into the face of the structure.

- Stakes should be placed at a 45-degree angle of each corner on the ground. Stakes that line up with any side will allow sway to occur on the other side. Also, never simply stake the tarp down through the grommets if avoidable. You should use stakes away from the tarp and cordage to connect the two.

- You should use knots (refer to the box above for the most common ones) that will stay secured but will also untie easily so you can adjust the setup if needed.

Tarp setup is no different than using natural materials. You can make setups that are good for one person or that will accommodate more than one. I will consider two for each scenario. Please keep in mind there are dozens of tarp setups, but in an effort to KISS it, I am going to discuss only a few. In this manner, you are not bogged down with tons of setups that you only know slightly well but rather have a few that you know very well. This goes back to the methods I taught in Section 1 on mind-set. You do not want to have too much running around in your head when you are under stress.

Tarp in a plow point setup, more visible with a signalling device and fire reflector to help protect fire.

ONE-PERSON SETUPS

CLASSIC V SETUP: The classic *V* setup is often referred to as the Boy Scout setup. For this setup, you need a ridgeline with rope or a downed tree. Place the tarp over the ridgeline with equal lengths of tarp on either side. Then stake the tarp down on all four corners.

WEDGE SETUP: With this setup, also called a plow point setup, you take one corner of the tarp and tie it to a tree or similar object about chest high. Then stake down the other three corners.

Both of these setups will comfortably cover one person, even two, if the tarp is big enough. You will have more head room with the wedge but will be covered more if you have the classic *V*. Just be sure that you do not put the face of the tarps into the prevailing winds. If you do, you will catch a large amount of wind, which will serve to cool you down.

TWO-PERSON SETUPS

LEAN-TO: This is no different than the natural-materials lean-to. With this setup, you have two corners tied to the ridgeline and two corners staked down. Prevailing winds should hit the back of the setup.

DOUBLE LEAN-TO: This setup assumes that you have at least two people with tarps. Face the lean-to setups toward one another so that you can build a fire in front of both. This way, any radiated heat from the fire goes into both the tarps and can be used to warm those inside of the lean-to.

GETTING COMFORTABLE WITHOUT CARRYING TOO MUCH WEIGHT

The key to staying comfortable without much weight is to know the things that will rob you of your heat. There are three things that will rob you of heat: wind, moisture and heat conduction away from the body. Knowing these three things will enable you to find gear pieces that will assist you in staying warm.

GARBAGE BAG: If you want to travel light, then put a garbage bag into your pocket. It can serve as a shelter, rain jacket and moisture barrier from the ground. You can fill it with wilderness debris such as pine needles and leaves to create a mattress.

REFLECTIVE BLANKET: These are indispensable devices to help keep you warm. They also pack up small enough to fit in a pocket. You can place them opposite you and the fire to reflect heat back to you. Place them around you like a wrap to hold and reflect heat, or lay them on the ground to reflect heat and keep you away from moisture.

PONCHO LINER (A.K.A. WOOBIE): Ask any veteran about their woobie, and most all of them will talk about its usefulness. The military-grade poncho liners have a unique polyester fiberfill that allows them to insulate incredibly well. They are always put together well and affordable at military surplus stores. They are called woobies because they were often a security blanket of sorts for scores of troops in the field.

GORE-TEX® BIVY: You can think of a bivy as a raincoat for your sleeping bag. Some are specific for sleep systems, such as the military sleep system. However, if you are wanting to travel light, then the Gore-Tex® bivy alone is a nice item that will shield you from wind and rain.

These are indispensable tools for being able to go to the wilderness with minimal gear. Remember, you start at the ground up with what clothes you wear and an understanding of how heat principles work.

PUT IT INTO PRACTICE

You probably already have a location where you can go to spend a night outside. Even if that location is hard to get to, if you have it available, you can do this practice in your backyard. As a matter of fact, I do that often when I am going to review and test out gear that I am unsure about. I will oftentimes sleep in it near the house. That way, if something goes awry or my equipment does not work as it should, I simply go inside.

➡ Tell someone that you plan on doing an overnight. Give them your proposed location and when they should expect to hear from you when you are done.

➡ Choose your favored tarp based upon my recommendations and go set it up in this location. Choose a night in which you will live but be uncomfortable with cooler temps. This way you are in no danger.

➡ Set up your tarp after practicing your knots at home and in the woods with the cordage you will use to set it up.

➡ Try out the sleep setup with leaves and a garbage bag. If you are new to this practice, take as much sleep gear as you wish. The more you practice, the more gear you should remove. Eventually get to where you can attempt an overnight in a squirrel's nest or primitive lean-to structure.

➡ Take mental or physical notes on what worked well and what did not work well. Next time you practice, make the necessary adjustments to fix what did not work.

CHAPTER 8

OBTAINING HEAT THROUGH FIRE AND FRICTION

NEXT TO KNOWING HOW TO DRESS WELL, FIRE IS ONE OF THE MOST IMPORTANT BUSH SKILLS THERE ARE, BECAUSE IT IS ONE OF THE FEW MEANS AVAILABLE TO MAKE UP MOST GREAT DEFICIENCIES.

—MORS KOCHANSKI

When you consider the American West, it has the reputation of being an incredible expanse of rugged wilderness ripe for those interested in outdoor recreation. Utah is one of those wonderful places in the American West that you can play soccer in a pair of shorts and a T-shirt in one location and in another, only a few miles away, there will be adventurers snowshoeing and riding snowmobiles.

It was there that a couple, a young British man and his American girlfriend, determined to rent a Jeep and go explore some of the more scenic but rough areas of the Utah mountains. While on a day trip of viewing the surroundings from their Jeep, it began to snow heavily at a high altitude in the mountains. This was not uncommon for this time of year. Being new to that terrain, the vehicle and the ability to drive in those conditions, the couple quickly got the Jeep stuck in the snow.

They had only the clothes they wore, which were blue jeans and sweatshirts. They had only the food they'd brought—some sunflower seeds and candies. They stayed in the vehicle for three days, eventually getting colder each passing day. Recognizing that with their abilities they would not be able to stay alive, they agreed to attempt a hike back to the nearest town, which was nearly 20 miles (32 km) away.

Very shortly after the hike began, the young lady became ill from the conditions and stress of the situation and could no longer go on. She convinced her boyfriend to go on without her. He reluctantly agreed and promised to come back with help. The young man was eventually found by local ranchers wandering through the wilderness a few days later. He was nearly exhausted, dehydrated and hypothermic. His presence was notified to SAR personnel, who had already started looking for them when it was discovered that the young man had not made his flight back to England.

The SAR crew found the young lady dead shortly thereafter. Tests revealed she died from hypothermia.

As with many of these stories, help was sent to the parties involved. It was only done after someone did not show up for work, missed a flight or something similar. As I have detailed so many times, *tell someone where you are going and when you expect to return.* That person will be able to notify others in a timelier fashion. In this particular instance, the authorities were detectives in Scotland Yard. They were notified when the young man missed his flight. They then checked his apartment and discovered credit card expenses and noticed they distinctly stopped one day. This was the day the couple got lost. They then notified authorities in the United States, who then initiated the search. This all took several days to complete.

For this particular chapter, I would also like to focus attention on the need for a fire. It is known that the Jeep did not run out of gas, but rather simply got stuck. With that information you can assume there was still fuel in the tank. Fuel that could have been used to start a fire even in wet conditions. Fuel could have been siphoned from the tank or a hole punctured in the gas tank. Siphoning gas is easy to do. You simply need to place any sort of tubing (from the engine or one you keep in your car kit) into the tank via the normal gas intake. You then need to suction hard with your mouth into the tubing. The gas will eventually come out due to suction. You will take some gas into your mouth and you will need to immediately spit that out and be prepared not to allow the gas from the hose to spill on you. Then, direct the gas coming out to a container or the area you want to make a fire. To puncture a hole in the tank is not difficult either. Any sharp instrument can be used and hammered into the tank. If you have trouble determining where your gas tank is, simply follow the gas spout to where the gas is deposited. Strike your sharp instrument into the tank by "hammering" it in with any sort of heavier object. Gather the fuel with a container or soak it up with a piece of clothing. You can then utilize that as an accelerant for the fire.

Regular gasoline (not diesel fuel) has a relatively low ignition point, which means it will catch fire with a flame or a spark. Just be careful that you build a fire away from the area in which you got your gas. The fumes from the gas are actually what light. If there are fumes that have settled all the way back to your main fuel source, then lighting the fumes will carry to it as well and could possibly cause a larger and more dangerous fire.

By doing these things, you will make the vehicle inoperable in short order. This is not a problem if it was already stuck and immovable. No change there then. You could easily use woody material from the area the young couple was in to fuel the fire. The spare tire could have been used as a signaling device. They were surrounded by snow. White smoke from a fire would have been hard to see by an airborne searcher. Black smoke emitted from a burning tire would have been much more visible. In this situation, they could have kept the tire by the fire and placed it on it if they heard an aircraft.

If they had a minimum of basic supplies in the vehicle, they would still be alive today. Those things could have included the following:

- Fire-starting material, lighter or ferrocerium rod. You could also start a fire by using two leads from the car battery to create sparks on the fuel gathered from the vehicle.

- Extra clothes in the case of an emergency. The young man was found wearing thin dress shoes like you might wear to work and two shirts, but no jacket, coat or mittens.

- Water bottles or similar containers. They were surrounded by snow, which means they had access to clean water. They could have melted it using a container from the vehicle.

- Blankets or sleeping bag in case the Jeep broke down as it did.

The best solution for them was to build a fire and stay in the Jeep. The Jeep would have provided wonderful shelter from the elements and a fire built strategically near it would have provided heat into it.

Some other things to consider if you find yourself in a similar event:

- Use the interior floor mats in front of the tires to help them get traction to start momentum forward to get out of the snow. Snow is incredibly slick; the mats will help curb that problem.

- Gather limbs, branches and other forest debris under the tires to help it become unstuck.

- If you own the vehicle, purchase some chains or similar tire treads that can easily be placed on if you get stuck.

- Keep a shovel in the vehicle to help dig debris that will provide traction and place it in the tire track line. A shovel will allow you to dig snow away from the vehicle as well.

- Cut or rip the seat covers to provide extra layers of clothing. Use the sponge material in the seats for insulation.

Some of you may remember the wonderful fire scene from the movie *Castaway*, starring Tom Hanks. In it, Hanks's character is able to make fire using what is commonly referred to as the fire plow method. Once he starts the fire he yells, "Fire! I made fire!"

Hanks's character rejoices for good reason. Fire is an incredibly important skill to have for any wilderness adventurer. Here is a short list of some things you can do with fire:

- Warm yourself

- Boil water that needs to be sterilized

- Cook your food

- Harden tools

- Make containers

- Ward off insects and dangerous animals

- Use as a signaling device

SCIENCE OF FIRE

You need three things to make a fire:

FUEL SOURCES: These can be natural or man-made materials, including accelerants that have petroleum in them.

IGNITION SOURCES: Examples of ignition sources include a lighter, ferrocerium rod, flint and steel, bow drill or hand drill. An ignition source is any item that assists you in exponentially increasing the temperature of the fuel source.

OXYGEN: It is all around us. Your fire lay and further setup will help determine how much oxygen it will get.

Tom Hanks's character was right to be excited. Fire comes right behind shelter in order of importance because it makes getting and keeping body warmth much easier to accomplish. The issue with making fire is that people allow it to be very ego driven. Experienced outdoors people and backyard barbecue people all know that if others are depending upon you to make a fire, it is easy to get embarrassed when you cannot get it done. That is why I like to remove the ego out of the equation and simply look at building a fire from the scientific perspective. When you cannot make a fire, or cannot make it well, you simply break down the science of it all.

Let's take a look at each of these pieces of the triangle in great detail. Understanding these will help any person, novice or advanced, develop better skills at fire building.

FUEL SOURCES

Experience has proven to me that your most likely problem area when starting a fire is the fuel source. From a strategic perspective, the thing that keeps fuel sources from working easily is moisture. When choosing your fuel sources, choose those that have no moisture in or on them. What I want to do with our fuel source selection is to set ourselves up for success. It does not mean that you cannot make fire with subpar materials. But if you have the time and opportunity to do so, let's get the best of the best. Here is a list of considerations when picking up fuel sources:

➡ Never pick items directly off the ground. The sun and wind help to dry materials out that are lying around. If something is lying directly on the ground, the bottom portion will not get as much sun exposure and will therefore hold moisture.

➡ Pick items that are hanging in the air. You will almost always find dead material hanging from a live tree. Use a stick to knock it down if you cannot reach it.

- When gathering material, make sure you are not getting green branches, sticks or other material. You should be able to break the materials cleanly and hear an audible snap. If you break a branch and it sticks together or does not snap, it is often still green or otherwise contains moisture.

- Gather materials that naturally have higher concentrations of flammable resins in them if they are available. Ask anyone who burns wood as their primary heat source and they will tell you that certain tree types always burn fast and hot. They are not very dense and that is why they burn so quickly. For survival, the resin will assist you in getting the fire going. Some good choices are cedar, birch, pine, hemlock and spruce.

- Fatwood is a most excellent choice if it is available. It is also referred to as "pine knot," "lighter wood," "heart pine" and many other regional names. Unlike deciduous trees (e.g., oak and maple) that die from the inside out, pines and cedars die from the outside and go in. This means that the resin will go both in and down (due to gravity). If you happen upon a fallen tree in which you can access the root ball, you have hit fuel source heaven. The center of the root ball, as well as the knots where branches meet the trunk, contain a higher concentration of the resin. They will burn much hotter due to the resin acting as an accelerant.

Those are some good ways to set yourself up for success. The size of the materials and how you go about assembling them are nearly as important as the materials themselves. Consider using a lighter to light a log. It would take a considerable amount of time to make this happen, wouldn't it? That is why you should invest a fair amount of time into gathering materials and prepping them before you start your fire. The size of the material is vitally important—you must start small. For many years, survival instructors have utilized the human hand as a reference point for gathering materials. You should gather material and place it on the fire setup (discussed on page 89) in the following order.

Start with paper-thin material for tinder, then add larger forest debris to sustain it.

FINGERNAIL THICKNESS: Usually referred to as tinder, sometimes as a tinder bundle, these are the first items you should ignite. One choice is scraped bark from dead trees. Cedar, birch, poplar and ash are good choices. You can also use grass or dead herbaceous material of any sort. These are materials that have green stems when alive, but when they are dead they break apart rather easily. Leaves are a common choice for most people, but please keep in mind that picking material from the ground will almost always have moisture. If you can, gather leaves that have fallen but are not in contact with the ground. Those that are completely dead but have not fallen from the tree yet will work (beech leaves are a good example). However, good, dry leaves burn so quickly that their usefulness is nearly negligible.

PINKY-FINGER THICKNESS: Once you have the tinder collected, you can start gathering materials that are of this size, provided that it is dry material. If it is a branch or stick, I will almost always remove the bark since it is on the outside and holds some moisture.

THUMB THICKNESS: Use the same considerations as above; just collect larger material.

WRIST THICKNESS: Use the same considerations as above; just collect larger material. However, do not concern yourself with making the material shorter in length. Movies and Hollywood have shown nicely sawn wood with neat little ends. That is wasted energy in survival. Let the fire cut the larger pieces for you. I typically put the tips in and slowly move them in or place the middle of the branch on the fire and let the fire "cut" it in half. This saves you energy. The concern for many is that the fire will run down the branch or log and outside the fire. Typically, this is not a reason for concern. It stops at the edge of the main fire.

The other very important issue to consider is how to gather material and how much material you should gather. A good practice is to get a bundle of each of these sizes about the diameter of a softball. Gather each of them, keeping them separate until they are needed. Do not lay them on the ground if at all possible. Lay them on a pack, log, rock or similar item to ensure they do not get moisture on them. This may be overkill, but in survival you do not just *want* success—you will *need* it to stay alive.

This is how you should gather fuel sources to get a fire started. Strategies and tactics for keeping it going (possibly overnight) will be discussed later in the text.

Man-made fuel sources come in an incredible range of design and chemical configurations. I have listed several here and included some thoughts on each:

FASTFIRE: These cubes are one of the best on the market for you to place in a survival kit. They have a low flash point, burn hot, are easy to break into small portions and burn when wet. They are also smokeless and odorless.

TRIOXANE: This comes as fuel sticks used by the U.S. military for many years to warm food before the invention of meal-ready-to-eat (MRE) heaters. These burn excessively hot but put off an odor that is not healthy to breathe in.

MAGNESIUM: This is often coupled with a ferrocerium rod. Magnesium has a high flash point but burns excessively hot when it is lit. It burns out rather quickly due to its high temperature. Magnesium is typically pressed incredibly dense, which makes it easy to carry. This also makes it difficult to scrape a large amount off to utilize it. It is mostly odorless and burns when it is wet.

Modern fuel sources serve as accelerant and/or sustain natural materials.

Always have multiple methods in knowledge and gear choices to start a fire.

ALCOHOL-BASED PRODUCTS: Hand sanitizer, mouthwash, med kit cleaners and other items containing alcohol are included in this category. Alcohol ignites rather easily and is also multiuse. Having multiple purposes outside of fire building is always a plus for survival packing. Various products have higher concentrations than others. I suggest trying yours out before adding it to your kit.

VEHICLE FUEL: I want to include this as well because some wilderness situations mean you may simply be lost near your vehicle. You can use many portions of your vehicle for your survival:

➡ Fuel from the tank is the obvious fuel source, I know; the question arises on how best to get it out. You can siphon it out using hoses that you either keep in your car kit or remove from the engine. You can also drill or puncture a hole in the tank itself. These methods will make the car inoperable. But in a dire situation where the car does not work, it can be a lifesaver.

➡ Tires burn incredibly hot and put off black smoke. Black smoke is what you need as a signal if you are surrounded by snow or light-colored vegetation.

➡ Once a fire is going, seat covers and padding can be added to create black smoke and make a fire bigger. I do think they would be better served as clothing in this situation, however.

MAKING FIRE IN THE RAIN

- Scrape off outer bark that is damp or wet.

- Baton wood to get to inner dry wood.

- Look under downed trees for dry material.

- Look in cavity trees for dry material.

- Create feather sticks from the inner portion of batoned wood. To do so, shave the wood thinly but leave the ends in tact, utilizing the stick as a single piece of tinder.

- Always take accelerants that work well in wet conditions.

- Have a covering over the fire, even if it is temporary, to ward off continued rain on the fire setup.

- Use fire lay to keep materials off the ground.

IGNITION SOURCES

Ignition sources come in a wide variety of styles as well. There are two broad categories I could place them into: primitive and modern.

PRIMITIVE IGNITION SOURCES

Do not kid yourself here. Primitive ignition sources are difficult at best and you must have lots of practice to effectively utilize them. They also require the user to have decent health and no injuries due to the nature of how you must articulate and use your body to affect their use. To be clear, though, I think practicing and learning how to use them teaches you much more than a simple ignition source. It teaches you patience, determination, how to study your material well and an understanding of the principles of fire. I am a fan of using and teaching primitive ignition sources as much as using them as an ignition source. There are many primitive methods that

Bow drill is useful if you have no gear, but is difficult to master.

were used by native peoples in a wooded wilderness setting. Most of the others were utilized in either an arid or jungle environment. I will look at the bow drill and hand drill due to the wilderness nature of this text.

BOW DRILL

A bow drill consists of a handhold, spindle, hearth/fireboard, bow and cordage. Reference the photo on page 85 to get a visual of a basic setup. With practice, you will find what size material works best for you. Let's break down a good starter kit, so you can get to work learning with it.

HANDHOLD: This needs to be very dense wood, rock or other material that does not break down easily. This will be used to hold the spindle in place but will also allow it to spin freely. You will need to find or make a handhold notch in which the spindle rides.

SPINDLE: The spindle needs to be about the thickness of your thumb and the length of your outstretched "aloha" sign using your thumb and little finger. A good approximation would be 8 inches (20 cm). It needs to be more sharpened on the upper portion so it spins freely and blunt on the lower portion so it digs and causes friction on the lower section. It should be rounded enough to spin by the cordage, but if it is too smooth the cordage will slide around it and not grab and move the spindle. The wood choice needs to be of medium density, meaning you should be able to put a dent into it if you press it with your thumbnail. Some good choices are basswood, cottonwood, cedar, willow and soft poplar.

HEARTH/FIREBOARD: This should be about the thickness of your thumb and longer than your foot. You will need to create a divot for the bottom portion of the spindle, and then cut out a "pie piece" for the dust to fall through. This wood choice needs to also be of medium density.

BOW: This needs to be about the length measured from your armpit to the end of your outstretched hand. It should have an actual "bow" curvature to it. This can be of any material you wish, but make sure it is stout enough to work while at the same time pliable enough to allow the cordage to accept the spindle.

CORDAGE: Natural choices of cordage are hickory bark, dogbane, milkweed and animal sinew. Other choices that you are likely to have on an outdoor trip are boot strings, paracord or shredded clothes. You will almost always need to braid natural materials to have enough strength.

Once you produce the materials, you will need to put them together and use them properly. Follow these twelve steps (if you are left-handed, reverse the sides):

1. Secure the cordage to the bow on both ends. This will need to be adjusted regularly, so ensure it can be untied easily.

2. Hold the bow and string in your right hand. Place the spindle on top of the string. Twist it into the string so that when it is in, it is on the outside of the bow. You may need to hold the bow with your armpit and use both hands to do this.

3. Place the bottom of the spindle in the divot created on the fireboard. This should be done so that the outer edge of the spindle is in line with the edge of the fireboard.

4. Place the handhold on top of the spindle.

5. Align your body so that your left foot holds the fireboard in place and your right knee is directly behind your left foot.

6. Use your dominant hand to move the bow forward and back in the divot, while the opposite hand holds the apparatus steady. You can use your shin as a brace for your left hand.

7. Create a burned-in section of the divot, noticeable from the wood darkening. Stop and cut out your pie piece. This pie piece should be about one-seventh of the diameter of the divot.

8. Start the process again. At this point, you are creating dust in the pie piece. It should be dark brown, which means it is not just scraping off but also getting warm in the process. Take your time and be patient here—you are only creating dust at this point.

9. Do this until the pie piece is filled to the bottom of the spindle cranking above it.

10. Once you make that connection, crank your bow drill harder and faster to build up heat. This often takes minutes, not seconds.

11. Once you can see that a fair amount of smoke is coming off and that the dust is getting heated, remove the spindle gently.

12. You can then place this dust, which is now a small coal, into a tinder bundle and slowly bring it to flame.

This process is much harder than simply reading these steps. Here are some pointers to help you:

USE YOUR SHIN AS THE BRACE. Most people will get tired if they simply hold it with their arm.

LIGHTLY TAP THE HEARTH TO GET THE COAL OUT. Never use your knife to push it out. The heat will immediately transfer to the metal of the knife and effectively extinguish the coal.

DO NOT START BLOWING THE COAL INTO FLAME WITH YOUR MOUTH. This puts moisture on the coal, which will help extinguish it. Move the tinder bundle back and forth with your arm to activate air across the coal and bundle. Once it starts to heat up and get material going, you can then utilize your breath.

HAND DRILL

Using a hand drill is harder to learn in my experience, but once learned it is much easier to do than a bow drill simply because you do not need to use so many different parts. A hand drill consists of a spindle and a hearth board.

SPINDLE: The spindle should be the diameter of your small finger and about the length of your arm.

HEARTH BOARD: This should be the thickness of your small finger.

FOLLOW THE SAME BASIC PROCEDURE AS THE BOW DRILL. Rather than spinning it with the bow and handhold, you will instead spin it with the palms of your hands placed on either side of the spindle. You will find it useful to move the spindle and at the same time slide your hands down it. This will ensure that you have plenty of pressure between the spindle and board, which will in turn create more friction and heat.

Frontiersmen used flint and steel, along with char cloth.

MAKING CHAR CLOTH

When making or finding char material make sure it is blackened and not just brown or tan.

→ Use an empty metal container (tin is a good choice and an aluminum can will work if that is all you have). A number of people like to use Altoids mint cans.

→ Punch, drill or otherwise puncture a small hole about the size of a nail head into the lid of the tin.

→ Choose 100-percent natural material to place in the tin. This can range from punk wood, grasses, bark, to 100-percent cotton clothing such as T-shirts. I have had a great deal of success with blue jeans.

→ Cut and shred the material into pieces and fill your container with them.

→ Put the tin into or on a heat source. In a wilderness setting, you can put this into an already existing fire. If you are at home, you can place this on a burner of your stove.

→ The material will begin to nearly burn, but not be destroyed because there will not be enough oxygen.

→ If you have flame coming out of the hole, put it out. There is too much oxygen entering and your material will be completely burned up.

→ If you see smoke, you are doing well. Let it continue to heat until there is no more smoke.

→ Pull it out of the heat source and let the tin cool.

→ Open the tin to find your char cloth.

MODERN IGNITION SOURCES

I tell people all the time that if Daniel Boone could have carried a lighter around in his pocket, he would have. For our purposes here, I will be considering what methods he did use as well as what resources you have available now.

1. Flint, chert and other incredibly dense rocks are so hard that when you strike high carbon steel against them, they will actually shave off small, nearly molten pieces of steel. Those are the sparks that you see when you strike flint and steel together. This is how frontiersmen and other near-modern people throughout the world got sparks to make a fire. Steels come in a wide range of sizes, shapes and styles. The key is to strike them at such an angle that you shave

HOW TO MAKE A FIRE

Gather all your materials and get your bundles of varying-sized material laid out and ready to go. If it is raining, you will often be able to find dryer materials underneath raised logs and dead trees, inside reachable nesting structures, under rock shelters or overhangs and any other place where prevailing winds and rain do not soak materials.

- Dig an *X*-shaped ditch in the earth that is about 1 inch (3 cm) deep. This will serve to allow oxygen to travel under the fire setup.

- Lay dried thumb-sized branches across the *X*, evenly spaced about 1–2 inches (3–5 cm) apart. I call this a fire raft.

- If you are using primitive means, you will want to transfer your coal to the tinder bundle by means of a piece of bark, leaf or similar item.

- If you have a sparking device, such as flint and steel or ferro rod, you will want to throw the sparks into the bundle and then wave the bundle into flame.

- If you have a lighter, lay your tinder material on the fire raft and place the next size of sticks around it. Light the tinder.

- With the tinder burning calmly, lay it on the fire raft and add sticks the next size up around and on top of it, evenly spaced so that oxygen can still get to the tinder. Using a tipi method or log cabin setup at this point serves no noticeable advantage.

- Once you see the woody stems catching fire, slowly add sticks one or two at a time until you have as large a fire as you desire.

off thin pieces of the steel, which heat up due to the friction of doing so. You can then "throw" the sparks coming off into some sort of tinder. Char cloth works especially well for this. Flint and steel is a good way to make fire, and they bridge the gap between primitive methods and modern methods. They throw enough sparks to utilize with incredibly dry material. It burns out fast, which makes it hard to work with a fuel source that is damp from rain or humidity.

2. Ferrocerium rods are typically referred to as ferro rods for short. They are a very popular choice in the prepper and survival community for good reason. They are rather easy to scrape and make incredibly hot sparks. They are often coupled with a magnesium fuel source to supply you with both fuel and ignition. Here are some helpful hints when using a ferro rod:

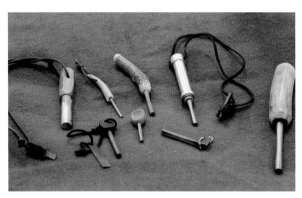

Ferro rods of various makes and models work in tough weather conditions to make sparks.

- Hold your scraper and pull your rod against it. This serves to concentrate your sparks a bit more and to direct them toward your tinder easier.

- Hold your scraper at less than 90 degrees to the ferro rod with the open face of the angle toward your tinder.

- Another method is to place the ferro rod directly into your tinder and hold it there steady. Then scrape down into your tinder. This has actually become my preferred method of utilizing one.

- If you have a brand new ferro rod, please realize they ship with a black coating on them. You will need to remove that coating before you utilize it.

3. Lighters—like cigarette lighters and fuel torches—all work virtually the same way. They are filled with a liquid fuel source. What actually burns at the nozzle is a vapor from the liquid. That vapor comes off easily if the lighter is warm, not well at all if it is cold. Therefore, you might need to use your body heat to get it warm enough to light.

4. Battery power is another modern ignition source. You can use the poles of your battery to heat up thin wires, which can in turn be used on dry tinder to get it ignited. You can also set your car jumper cables on your vehicle battery. Strike the cable ends together to create sparks.

5. Solar lenses come in many shapes and sizes. Start by placing your lens very near your tinder. The lens should be at 90-degrees relative to the sun. Slowly pull the lens away until you get the bright focal point on the tinder itself. One surprising method for creating a lens is to take your eyeglasses and utilize them in concert with water. Place a small amount of water on the face side of your glasses. This will create the convex shape needed on that side; the glasses themselves create the convex shape on the other side. Convexity on both sides is the way I utilize this type of lens. Another method is to take a piece of ice that is made with clear water and form it into a lens with the warmth of your hands. You can then make fire utilizing ice. It works as a nice party trick for you and your friends.

There are dozens more fire-ignition sources. For survival, I like to show the methods that are easy to create, especially under stress and possible injury. In Chapter 15, I will show you the gear pieces that go with you each and every day and the larger fire-starting kits I use.

Have plenty of wood that is long to allow you to feed your fire from your shelter.

STRATEGIES FOR KEEPING A FIRE GOING ALL NIGHT LONG

It might be that you only need a fire to boil some water or cook some food. If that is the case, there is no need to keep a fire going until you are rescued or you determine you need to leave and self-rescue. If you need to stay an entire night, there are several things you can do to keep it going.

The first is that you need to gather material before you stop for the night. Moving around after dark is dangerous for several reasons, so you should avoid it if possible. My rule of thumb is to gather a pile of material that you think will burn all through the night. Then gather that same amount of material twice more. This is one of the biggest surprises to those that are new to fire building. It takes a considerable amount of material to keep it going all night long. You may be fortunate to have pieces that are much larger in diameter. Keep in mind that you do not need to cut any material into cute little logs. This is only needed on TV shows and movies. In the real world, where your strategies mean life or death, you do not need to waste your energy making those cuts with a saw.

Second, set some material such that you can push them into the fire from within your shelter setup. This will keep you out of possible bad weather.

Last, you can practice what is referred to as a long fire. Long fire setups are made so that the heat radiated from the fire is near the length of your body rather than just one location. Spread coals from a larger fire the length of your body directly in front of your shelter. Place more sticks along the coals so they burn and form more coals. Keep placing material on the fire to keep making a long fire and more coals. This will allow you to lay in your shelter and get warmth from your feet all the way to your head. If you have multiple people in the shelter, you will need to trade spots from time to time for others to get warmed.

The question arises: What happens if the fire goes out, or it gets too big? The answer is simple: if you get too cold, you will wake up. The fire will still have some coals that you can easily blow back to flame with other material. If the fire gets too big, you will wake up and can then spread it out in such a way as to damper it a bit.

PUT IT INTO PRACTICE

It is time to start "playing with fire." Although I say that sort of tongue in cheek, I am also serious in that I want you to make fire as much and as often as you can. There is a progression to doing so. You will find yourself along this progression somewhere. Wherever you find yourself, jump in and continue growing your skill set.

➡ If you are new to fire making, I advise you to first learn the components individually. Start with the ignition starters—buy various lighters and practice with them. Ask yourself if you can use them if you are injured. Can you use them with your nondominant hand? Determine how to make them work in those situations. Once you do that, move on to ferrocerium rods.

- Next, buy some man-made fuel sources as discussed in this chapter. Use one of your easy-to-use ignition sources to ignite it. Note how long it burns, how hot it feels from a distance. Soak it in water—what happens when you try to light it then?

- Next, begin testing out natural materials for fuel sources. Gather various grasses, leaves, bark, woody stems, tree material and whatever else you want to burn. Avoid toxic species such as poison ivy, sumac or similar plants. Ignite them with your easiest-to-use ignition source. Note how easy or difficult it is to get lit. Commit to memory the materials that are easiest to light and learn how to find them easily.

- Do the same thing with not-so-easy-to-use sources. Sometimes it is easy to get frustrated once it gets harder. Don't allow that to happen. At this point, you are not needing it to survive— you're just practicing and learning. Be okay with that. I often tell my students that failure is simply success spelled backward. Once you feel comfortable doing this, then do the same thing on an overnight trip where you will need a fire for warmth, boiling water or cooking food.

- Build yourself a fire utilizing the methods I taught you in this chapter. Gather various woody sources and see if you can note the difference in how much heat they put off. This is not easy to do, but attempt it.

- After practicing this many times, plan on having climate-appropriate clothing and sleep gear. Attempt to sleep with a long-pole fire to keep you warm. Do so by wearing the right clothes but sleeping on top of your sleep gear. In this manner, if things do not go well, you will have the right gear to stay warm.

- Once you get comfortable with these modern sources, it is then time to start utilizing primitive and near-modern methods like a bow drill, flint, steel and others. Make the materials at home and practice there (or nearby where you can do so).

- Once you can do these comfortably, it is time to go into the woods and harvest materials and then do the primitive methods on the spot. I would still suggest taking your own cordage, as it is the hardest of a bow-drill set to manufacture in the wilderness in a timely fashion.

- Once you are comfortable with that, then make your own cordage or move on to a hand drill, fire bow or the methods the native people from your area used. Every area is different, but native peoples were masters at understanding their environment. Study how they did it and practice what they used.

Now that I have you being triumphant with fire, much like Tom Hanks was in *Castaway*, it is time to move on through our Rule of Three. You have taken care of what I would consider our immediate needs, which are personal safety and core body temperature. You now must take of your hydration needs. It may seem simple, but carrying or procuring water is not as easy as you may think.

CHAPTER 9

PROCURING CLEAN WATER

THE BEST PLACE TO CARRY WATER IS IN YOUR STOMACH.
—ANONYMOUS SGT., UNITED STATES ARMY SPECIAL FORCES

White Sands National Monument in New Mexico holds an otherworldly beauty for those who wish to visit. Its rolling sand dunes are beautiful, inspiring and, as deserts always are, very unforgiving. In the summer of 2015, a fifty-one-year-old woman, her forty-two-year-old husband, and their nine-year-old son visited White Sands for a short hike to take in some of the beauty. The temperatures were hovering slightly above 100°F (38°C) on that day, which was normal for that time of year.

The family had no experience hiking in a desert. The woman began the hike with a knee that had been previously injured and was giving her problems. The family started off with 40 ounces (1.2 L) of water divided between two water bottles, one carried by the woman the other carried by the man.

Shortly after the hike started on a well-marked 4.6-mile (7.4-km) loop trail, the family left it and went down one of the dunes. It is unknown if this was an accidental or purposeful act. The woman aggravated the knee even further, and coupled with not feeling well, determined she should go back to the car. This occurred 1 mile (1.6 km) into their hike. The man and his son continued on.

Shortly after leaving, the woman was overcome by the heat and exposure and collapsed 984 feet (300 m) from where she left her husband and young son. The man and his son continued, unaware of the fate of his wife. A mere 1,969 feet (600 m) more, the father also collapsed from similar issues.

Five hours after the start of the hike, while on regular patrol, park service employees found the body of the woman. Upon a quick investigation, they discovered pictures of her husband and the boy on her phone and made a hasty search. They discovered the young boy sitting next to the body of his father. An autopsy performed later confirmed their suspicions that they both died from heat-related illness exasperated by their severely dehydrated state. It is known that they offered more water to their son than they took themselves.

Let's take a look at how you could handle it if you happen to be in this situation in the future. There are three key issues you can change to achieve a different outcome. The family had:

1. little to no knowledge of the area in which they were hiking;

2. no method or gear available to shield themselves from the heat; and

3. not enough water to keep themselves functioning in this environment.

The first issue can easily be solved by a small amount of research before you head out. With the Internet and its vast amount of knowledge available, you can easily find out information such as the length of a hike as well as shelter and water availability. Particularly when it comes to government-owned land, there are a number of online resources and even brochures at many of the trailheads and visitor centers when those locations and personnel are available.

One of the things that is often overlooked when utilizing the resources is the posted warnings. These warnings are in place for good reason. Most likely, someone else was injured or died in the area and the authorities posted signage or information to make others aware of the danger. *Heed these warnings!* They are there for your safety.

Upon a cursory glance at available information, this family should have known that there were absolutely no natural or man-made shelters available along this trail. That does not mean that you cannot go into such an area, it just means that you must have something that can provide you with some shelter in the case of an emergency. A light, long-sleeved shirt and wide-brimmed hat can easily shield you from a fair amount of the sun's rays. If the material is cotton, then it also serves to hold moisture against your body, which will help to cool your body temperature in that type of environment. A reflective blanket is also a good choice in such a situation. Note, though, that a reflective blanket is not to be used in the same manner you would use one for hypothermia. Actually, it's used in just the opposite way. Reverse it so that the reflective side is toward the sun and the nonreflective side is toward your body. This way, much of the sun's heat is reflected away from you.

Last, and most important, is the need for water. You should have close to 1 gallon (3.8 L) of water per day. That is why the quote at the beginning of this chapter is so important to understand. Special forces soldiers do not wait until they need water to start drinking it. It is imperative that they stay hydrated at all times so they can be ready for whatever may come their way. This is a good example for all of us. Before going on any outdoor excursion, hydrate as you are going there. Then take as much water as you can comfortably carry with you when you leave. This can easily be done with a small daypack that has water bottles in it, a hydration bladder or a belt-carried canteen pouch. In this manner, you start the trip hydrated and you hydrate along the way.

That should give you a good understanding of three simple ideas that could have helped in this real-world scenario. Now, let's take an in-depth look at water and why many sources of water are no longer drinkable, how to fix that problem and much more.

THE NEED FOR WATER AND WHY IT IS SO IMPORTANT

Our bodies are made up mostly of water. Consider these facts:

➡ The adult human body is 65 percent water.

➡ Blood is 95 percent water.

➡ Brain and muscle tissue are 75 percent water.

SIGNS OF DEHYDRATION

MILD

➡ **Thirst due to dry mouth**

➡ **Headaches**

➡ **Muscle cramps**

➡ **Low urine output**

➡ **Dry skin**

MODERATE

➡ **Dizziness**

➡ **Dark urine or no urine output**

➡ **Poor skin elasticity**

➡ **High rate of heartbeat and breathing**

➡ **Irritability**

SEVERE

➡ **Unconsciousness**

➡ **Seizure**

➡ **Death**

Couple those facts with the understanding that you do not create water within your body. If you are not getting water, there is simply no way that your body can function properly. Your body needs water for thermoregulation, digestion, circulation and transportation of body contaminants out through sweat, urination and defecation.

In a survival situation, you not only need water for the purpose of hydration to accomplish all these bodily functions properly, but you also need it for proper hygiene and food preparation. Now that you understand the need and how to recognize it, let's take a look at the contaminants found in water and then find ways to get them out.

Depending upon your body size, to function properly your body needs between ½ gallon to 1 gallon (1.9 L to 3.8 L) of water each day. That is what you need to be normal. In a survival situation, which is far from normal, you can live on less but your goal should be to get this suggested amount. Pay attention to your sweat as well. If you are sweating profusely, you will need to replace that water. Don't forget what I have told you—survival is a lazy person's game. Your goal is to not use up any more water or calories than you have to.

WATERBORNE CONTAMINANTS

There are four main sources of waterborne threats that pose a problem to humans when they make their way into the human body:

PROTOZOAN: These are the most common contaminants. Giardia and cryptosporidium are the biggest culprits. Symptoms are diarrhea, stomach cramps, weight loss (in longer-term problems) and severe fatigue. The incubation period (how long protozoa take to start causing problems after entering the body) is quite varied. Giardia typically takes over a week to two weeks, whereas cryptosporidium can set up and cause issues within a few days.

VIRAL: These are another common type of contaminants that you can experience. These include Rotavirus, enterovirus and hepatitis A. You will notice a fever, fatigue, diarrhea, nausea and vomiting. Incubation times vary greatly and are dependent upon the particular virus. Some set up as quickly as one day, others may take a full month.

BACTERIAL: These are not very common. Bacteria, such as Salmonella and E. coli, are indicated by diarrhea, abdominal pain, nausea and vomiting. Depending upon your health and the amount of bacteria, you can start experiencing problems from one day to two weeks after taking them in.

CHEMICAL: There is no standardization of understanding of how chemical contaminants will affect us. Their origins are incredibly broad (such as agricultural runoff, industrial waste and human-waste runoff). This also includes far-reaching problems such as biological or nuclear fallout or their waste.

Unless you find yourself in a large metropolitan area, the easiest way to get clean water is to gather what falls from the sky. This includes dew, rain, snow and ice. These sources, along with condensation, can be considered clean and drinkable. The only issue is gathering it efficiently for your use.

DEW

Dew is easily gathered by taking a bandana and utilizing it as a makeshift sponge. In the early morning hours, when dew is the heaviest, simply wipe down any vegetation that is not toxic (see sidebar below) and wring what you gather into your mouth. You can also easily tie the bandana to the lower portion of your leg and drag it through grass and weeds (again, avoid toxic species) and wring that into your mouth as well.

TOXIC SPECIES TO AVOID

 POISON IVY: "Leaves of three, stay away from me" is true. Poison ivy contains urushiol, which is an oil that can cause severe dermatitis. If ingested, it can cause an allergic reaction in the mouth and throat, leading to swelling and possible suffocation.

 POISON HEMLOCK: Ingesting any part of this plant will most likely lead to death.

 BUTTERCUPS: Sounds like a wonderfully nice name, doesn't it? However, all parts of this plant can severely damage your digestive system.

 NIGHTSHADE: All parts, especially the berry, can be fatal. It causes intense disturbance and pain in both the digestive and nervous systems.

 JIMSONWEED: Indicators of ingestion of this plant are abnormal thirst, delirium, then coma.

IN JUNE 1995, U.S. Military Pilot Scott O'Grady was shot down by opposing Bosnian-Serb forces. O'Grady evaded capture for several days, sometimes with the enemy only a few feet from his position. He leaned heavily on the skills he learned in SERE school. One such skill was utilizing a sponge from his survival kit to soak up rain and dew and store it in plastic bags for consumption later. This action kept him hydrated so he could use military equipment and procedure to notify an American pilot that he was alive and needing extract. The United States Marines were happy to take care of that for him.

RAIN

Rain is a glorious thing when it comes to survival, if you can keep yourself dry. As you discovered in Chapter 7, a good tarp is a must-have piece of equipment that goes to the field with you each time you go out. If it is raining, simply take a look at your tarp after it is set up. Gravity and the manner in which you set it up will create folds that carry water in certain directions off of the tarp. If your setup is incredibly tight, then allow some slack in it so that these folds are created. Once you have noticed a spot where a fair amount of water is running off, then drink straight from that stream. If you have a container, such as your water bottle, place it at the end of the stream and gather water. In this manner, you do not have to place yourself outside while drinking the water. Gather it, take it back to your shelter and drink inside the shelter.

You can also use an indentation in the earth. Line it with a garbage bag or tarp and allow it to be a makeshift rain catcher. The indentation can be natural or man-made. Depending upon the rate at which the rain is falling, you can easily get more than adequate amounts of water in a short amount of time.

SNOW AND ICE

One of the largest misunderstandings in the survival community is that you should never take in snow or ice. If you are in the process of setting up shelter, gathering firewood, setting traps or hunting, then you are going to be moving about and your body temperature is going to rise. It is at this time that you can easily gather snow or ice and ingest it. It is best to melt it in your water bottle rather than taking it directly to your mouth. Place some in your water bottle and keep it inside your outer layer of clothing. Your body heat will not be compromised and that heat will serve to melt the snow and ice. Please note that you should not be attempting this hydration strategy if you are sitting in a shelter. If that is the case, your body temperature is not naturally higher. This act will serve to lower your body temperature and start you down the path of hypothermia.

CONDENSATION

Condensation is an option, but there is a reason it is last here. If everything goes well with the methods listed below, you will still only get minimal amounts of water. That is much better than no water, so I need to discuss it. In both of these methods, you are going to gather and collect evaporated water particles:

TRANSPIRATION BAGS are easily put together and use very little energy on your part to get water. Simply take a clear plastic bag and place it over vegetation (e.g., tree leaves, bushes, grass) that you know are not toxic. Tightly tie the end of the garbage bag off at its opening. Then sit back and wait. If there is ample amount of sunlight, naturally occurring evaporation will occur. Once it comes off of the plant it cannot escape the bag. Let this sit for a minimum of 24 hours, then gather what water is inside. I do this in my survival basics classes and have gotten as much as 2 cups (480 ml) of water from a tree.

Let nature gather water by using a transpiration bag on living vegetation like this sycamore branch.

SOLAR STILLS require a lot of work and yield very little water. I do think this method is still important to know because it is one of the few that work in an arid environment or in an area where there is no vegetation. To make a solar still, dig a circular pit 8–12 inches (20–30 cm) deep and 2–3 feet (60–90 cm) across. Place a container in the center of the pit. Fill up the pit with anything that has water in it. This could include water from an unclean source, vegetation and even urine. Place a bag or tarp over the pit and secure it outside of the pit area with stakes or rocks. Place a stone or similarly weighted object on top of the bag so that it creates a funnel directly over the top of the container. Inside the pit, water will, over several hours, evaporate and rise to the bottom of the tarp. Gravity will pull it toward the center, where it will fall off and into the container you place to catch it. I want to emphasize, as stated in Chapter 1, survival is a lazy man's game. If this setup requires you to use more water than you are gathering, you are making your situation worse by doing it. This is not a favorite method of mine, as it often requires you to expend more water than you receive from building it. In an arid environment, where the ground is much softer, it does not take as much effort to build this setup. It is there that a solar still will be a viable option.

Drilling a hole with your knife or completely severing a grapevine in the spring will provide you with clean water.

If you must drink water from a stream, choose moving water downstream of moss.

GRAPEVINE

Wild grapevine is a great choice for getting water, but it is dependent upon the season. When the natural processes of biology are pushing water into the vine (spring and summer growth season), clean drinkable water is easy to obtain. Simply cut a notch in the vine. I prefer to cut a *V*-shaped notch with the bottom of the *V* on the lower side of the vine. This will allow water to come out of the vine and gravity will pull it to the bottom of the *V*. Gravity will then further pull it toward the earth, where you can then place your mouth or, preferably, a container of any sort. It will come out in drips and you can easily get 1 cup (240 ml) of water in less than an hour during peak growing season. Grapevine will grow near the trunk of a tree and will grab the tree only by the curvature of the vine itself. Poison ivy will have a growth from it that looks like small hair that attaches directly to the tree itself. There are also other vine species that have a similar look, but do not produce water like wild grape. To be safe, only utilize a species that grows without what appears to be hair on it.

RUNNING WATER

All running water on the earth can possibly contain contaminants. Scientists have found contaminants in harsh, cold environments with very little intervention from animals, including humans, in Antarctica. That does not mean that all water sources are poor choices. The following are some best management practices for getting the best water possible:

➡ Go to the source of where it comes out of the ground. The longer a stream of water runs on the earth's surface, the more opportunity for contaminants to enter it.

➡ Go to a high spot on a hill to do this. Water runs downhill. If you can find a spring that starts higher on the hill, you will again have found one which has less opportunity for contaminants to run into it underground. In general, the best method to search for water is to go downhill first. Find where water is running, then follow it to the source.

- Choose downstream from moss. Moss will act as a poor substitute for a filter but it is better than no filter at all. Many contaminants will get caught up in the moss and not pass downstream.
- Choose water that is moving, not sitting still. Very poor choices are ponds and puddles.

BOILING WATER WITH ROCKS

I will look at using modern tools when boiling in the next section. However, a primitive method to boil water is to make a pot of clay in the earth and fill it with water. Then add hot rocks from a nearby fire to it so that you bring it to a boil. While this is incredibly primitive, it may be the only method you are left with, especially if you have no container to boil in.

Boiling water is a near fool-proof method for cleaning water.

PROCESSING WATER WITH USEFUL TOOLS

If you are going to take gear with you, there are a number of items you can use to filter and further decontaminate the water:

STAINLESS STEEL WATER BOTTLE: Most everyone that ventures outside takes a water bottle with them. Choose a stainless steel option so that if you need to you can also easily use it to boil other water sources you gather from the environment. Despite the overwhelming amount of Internet "evidence" to the contrary, you can assume that water that is brought to a rolling boil is safe to drink. You do not need to adjust your methods based upon altitude or let the water boil for several minutes.

CARBON: Understanding science is a wonderful thing. A Dutch scientist, Johannes Diderik van der Waals, discovered that certain molecular structures have attractive or repulsive forces when they come in contact with one another. One of these is that most waterborne contaminants are attracted to the molecular structure of carbon, whereas water molecules are not. Therefore, when you pour or pull water through a carbon filter, those contaminants will not pass through and the water will. Water filter companies seized upon this and created any number of products that utilize a carbon filter as the main component of a water filtration straw or pump.

A personal filter straw, Sawyer® Mini is shown, is a must-have gear item.

For family units or teams, a water pump, Katadyn® hiker PRO is shown, is a needed gear item.

CERAMIC FILTER STRAWS: Seizing upon this same scientific process, other companies manufactured materials into man-made filters that do the same thing.

PUMPS: Similar in makeup to the ceramic straws, pumps are made much larger and use a pump alongside so that you can place one tube into an unknown water source and pump water into your container via the output tube on the other end.

IODINE DROPS AND TABLETS: Iodine drops do not remove the contaminants from a water source. They do, however, make them inert. A two-percent tincture is required to be an effective solution. You must use these sparingly. Only one to two drops are needed for 1 quart (1 L) of water. Any more than that and you could easily cause organ damage for yourself. More is *not* better with iodine.

CHEMICAL DROPS AND TABLETS: There are many makers of other chemical additives. They work much the same way that iodine does in that they do not remove contaminants, they simply make them inert and they then pass through your digestive track without doing you harm.

STERILIZING PENS: These are devices that work on batteries and emit UV light. You utilize them by placing the light into the container of water and stirring it around. The UV light does not "kill" the bacteria; rather, it makes them inert.

There is so much information out there when considering these options. Please consider the following table to assist you in understanding the options available. Also note that the Ease of Use Under Stress category considers someone who is lost, making poor decisions and possibly injured. These are attributes of those that are in a real-life survival scenario rather than just training for one or otherwise camping. I graded each of these sections excellent, good, fair or poor.

WATER FILTRATION SYSTEMS

FILTRATION SYSTEM	EFFECTIVENESS UNDER STRESS	TYPICAL USEFULNESS	EASE OF USE UNDER STRESS	COST (USD)
Stainless steel water bottle	Excellent	Excellent	Fair	10–20
Carbon filter	Good	Fair	Excellent	10–15
Ceramic filter	Good	Good	Excellent	15–20
Pumps	Good	Good	Good	>75
Iodine drops	Poor	Good	Poor	<5
Chemical drops	Poor	Good	Poor	<10
Sterilizing pens	Poor	Poor	Poor	>75

In summary, it would be my opinion that you have a multi-tiered approach, which would include:

➡ each person carrying their own stainless steel water bottle;

➡ each person carrying their own ceramic filter; and

➡ one person in a group carrying a water pump.

This will allow each individual to carry water with them in the bottle, and when it runs out they can easily filter water on the individual level. When the need arises to set up a base camp, you can then use a pump to gather a large volume of water more easily.

HONORABLE MENTIONS WHEN CLEANING WATER

Besides the methods just discussed, there are additional (albeit more unusual ways) to gather water:

PLASTIC BOTTLE: You can boil water in a plastic bottle. The key is to not put the bottle directly in the flame. The heat will transfer from the bottle to the water due to heat conduction. If there are any bubbles between the flame and the water, they will not conduct heat. You will experience a hole burned through at that location.

CONDOM: This works in the same way as a plastic water bottle. I recommend carrying one simply because they are light, take up little space and can also be used for other purposes.

HILLBILLY WATER FILTER: Create your own carbon filter by utilizing anything that is hollow, such as a discarded water bottle. Fill it with carbon pieces from an old fire, a tree struck by lightning and so on. Use a bandana or shirt to filter the water before it goes in and as it is coming out. You do not want to digest loose carbon particles as they will make you vomit.

MOISTURE FROM EDIBLE PLANTS: Those plants you are eating that are juicy are good choices to get water as well. Chickweed and purslane are good examples of edibles that are very juicy.

NO URINE: I must mention it simply because survival TV has depicted this so many times. Under no circumstances should you drink any urine. Urine is the portion of what you ingest that your body determines it needs to rid itself of. You are in essence placing concentrated toxins back into your body. It makes for marketable television shows but sick survivalists.

I have gone into great detail and given you many choices when it comes to water. Experience has shown that it is the most overlooked aspect of not only survival preparedness but daily living as well. It is estimated that as many as 75 percent of Americans suffer from chronic dehydration. Add to that fact that very few Americans suffer from chronic hunger. This is because hunger pains are often answered by eating food. Eating serves to further dehydrate us. Much water is needed to process food. Hunger pains are often actually dehydration pains. They are your body telling you it is dehydrated. Most are simply not aware of the multiple warning signs that the body gives off to indicate being dehydrated. Be mindful of your body and what it is telling you.

CHAPTER 10

UNDERSTANDING YOUR ENERGY NEEDS AND HOW TO OBTAIN THEM

CHANCE FAVORS THE PREPARED MIND.

—LOUIS PASTEUR

Mushrooms. They are often colorful reminders of cartoons with Smurfs and other little make-believe creatures. Unfortunately, these cute little fungi can be incredibly deadly.

One young man, aged 29, traveled into the wilderness on a simple day hike to enjoy all that nature has to offer. He found what appeared to be an appetizing mushroom and gathered as many as he could find to take home. He then asked his girlfriend to cook them for dinner for him and his family, which included two of his sisters and his seventeen-month-old child.

Shortly after eating the dinner, the family members starting hallucinating, vomiting and having severe stomach pains. After only a few hours, the young man's girlfriend had died from eating the mushrooms, and over the next two days each of the people who ate them, including the child, succumbed to the poisonous toxins that were found in them.

The question begs to be asked: Can you eat mushrooms? Yes, certainly you can eat mushrooms. If your desire is to homestead and live a more natural lifestyle, there are many variations of mushrooms that are tasty, nutritious and filling. The vast majority of them simply do not have enough carbohydrate or nutrition to warrant their use in a survival-related event, however. In addition, keep in mind that in a stressed survival-related event, you are not making sound decisions. Harvesting of mushrooms, and any wild edible for that matter, is dangerous without sound knowledge. I recommend people stay completely away from mushrooms during survival situations. Some common edible varieties, such as morels, can become toxic simply by what host they grow on.

In short, for survival, stay completely away from mushrooms. There is not enough food value there to take the risk.

HOW MANY CALORIES AND WHAT SORT OF NUTRITION DO YOU NEED?

As I begin this subject, let's make sure to understand at the beginning that I am talking about survival. I am not talking about abundant living, an exercise regimen, or lack thereof, or homesteading. You need to understand how your body works, how much food you actually *need* to stay alive, as well as strategies for obtaining it.

The time to get healthy, properly hydrated and other related nutritional needs is now. Do not wait until you are thrust into a survival situation to have a need to get into shape and be healthy. I discussed this in Chapter 9 with water. The best place to store water is in your stomach. The same goes for nutrition. The best place to store nutrition is in your body. Just like water, that is a temporary solution if your needs are going to last into

the days and weeks. There have been situations where humans miraculously survived several weeks without eating any food during the Haiti earthquakes. It should be obvious that they did not have energy to do anything. They will have negative health effects for years to come.

Let's take a look at the average person, and you can base your needs on what you see from them:

➡ The average male in the United States is 5 feet 10 inches (175 cm) tall and weighs 196 pounds (89 kg).

➡ The average female in the United States is 5 feet 5 inches (165 cm) tall and weighs 145 pounds (66 kg).

We will consider how the following processes effect an intake of 100 calories. The game of calories and nutrition in and out of your body is the key to staying alive. Remember, as I have said many times, survival is a lazy person's game. This means the more calories you expend, the more you have to make up. Therefore, have as little caloric expenditure as you can. Here are the ways that calories get burned:

➡ Activity

➡ Eating and digesting food

➡ Bodily processes and functioning

ACTIVITY

Any time you move, you are burning calories. The more you stress your muscles, the more calories you will burn. This works great for exercise, but it's not good at all for survival. This is why I have recommended strategies for building shelters, burning fires and other activities in which you do as little as possible. Light physical activity, such as tying up a shelter and gathering leaves, will burn about 20 percent of your calories that you utilize in a day. Something as vigorous as cutting firewood with an ax could easily burn 40 percent of the calories you have in a day.

EATING AND DIGESTING FOOD

This is really easy to overlook and very important in the overall strategy of survival. When you chew food and send it through the digestive process, you burn a lot of calories. What you eat will determine how many calories that is. If you are eating plant material, that is about 10 percent of your daily caloric burn. If you are eating solid meat protein, you are burning upward of 40 percent of your caloric needs. Suffice it to say, edible plants need to be understood along with hunting and trapping strategies.

BODILY PROCESSES AND FUNCTIONING

Consider your lungs working, your heart beating, thermoregulation and more. Even at complete rest and sleep, your body still does these things; therefore, it is burning calories to do it. Just keeping you alive is going to use a very large amount of your calories (some studies show as much as 60 percent). There is nothing you can do to slow, minimize or otherwise limit this calorie use. You must be in the process of getting calories when and where they happen.

BASAL METABOLIC RATE

Your basal metabolic rate (BMR) is the number of calories your body requires to maintain its current weight. Keep in mind most Americans are overweight, so there is some body fat to spare. When your body goes into starvation mode, it is unhealthy. While you can survive 8–21 days without any food or water (albeit with long-term health problems), some studies suggest you can survive several weeks without food if you have ample water. You want to avoid this if possible. The Mifflin-St. Jeor equation will help you calculate your BMR based upon you specifically. This is one of those items we need to use to educate ourselves now, so we have this knowledge if we need it later in survival situations. I am not suggesting you make these calculations in the field during a survival event. Use your weight in kilograms, your height in centimeters and your age in years for this equation.

(YOUR WEIGHT X 9.99) + (6.25 X YOUR HEIGHT) - (4.92 X YOUR AGE) + 5 FOR MEN

(YOUR WEIGHT X 9.99) + (6.25 X YOUR HEIGHT) - (4.92 X YOUR AGE) - 161 FOR WOMEN

Once you do this calculation, you will arrive at the number of calories you need to stay at the weight you currently are. Basic bodily functions will require a fair amount of calories; it is important to get working on calories as soon as possible. (Not to mention the simple morale boost that eating will bring.)

OVERALL STRATEGY

Understanding that you can actually live for weeks without food is important in the list of priorities. Due to its nature of helping you become more productive and the morale boost it serves, getting food as soon as possible is important. Rationing food is vital to your survival. Since the majority of most search-and-rescue operations are less than five days, you should immediately ration food for that many days. This should also give you enough energy to attempt to find calorie and nutrition sources from your environment.

FORAGING AND GATHERING EDIBLE PLANTS

Nutritionists have discovered that eating and digesting plant material requires much less expenditure of calories. The study of edible wild plants is a broad one based upon the region in which you live. It is also a study that must begin now, so you have the skill when you need it. I will take a look at how to go about studying edible wild plants and then consider some broad categories of foods that are found in most wildernesses:

➡ Find edible plant classes in your area. You can easily do an Internet search for "wild edible plants class" and find some that are specific to your area.

➡ Obtain a minimum of three good resources to begin your study of edible plants. I recommend three because a study of wild edible plants can become a very regional practice. Some resources are more detailed than others. I highly recommend choosing a book that has illustrations rather than photos. There is so much randomness and variance in how plants look that an artist is better at capturing the elements needed for your study than a photographer will be by photographing one species. My recommendations are:

➡ *Identifying and Harvesting Edible and Medicinal Plants in Wild (and Not So Wild) Places* by Steve Brill and Evelyn Dean;

➡ *A Field Guide to Edible Wild Plants* by Lee Allen Peterson; and

➡ *Botany in a Day* by Thomas Elpel.

➡ When you start your study, plan on discovering one or two plants on any given trip. Plan on finding them over and over on that day. Your efforts in study need to be focused upon imprinting this information in your brain. If you go with one or two, then you will be able to more adequately do this. Most people attempt to go out and identify every species they see. This method does not work for imprinting for future use.

➡ Sketch as many plants as you can. This further helps you to imprint the information. By so doing, you purposely note whether stems are round or square; leaves are opposite or alternating; blooms are swirled or otherwise. Please know you do not have to have great sketching ability. This is not something you will share. It serves to help you by keeping the information in your head.

Those resources are all exhaustive resources on the topic. For basic survival methodology, I want to focus on what our nutritional needs are. You cannot live on protein alone. Here are our needs and various species that will help you get them in the wild:

CARBOHYDRATE: Think of carbohydrate as the best way to quickly add energy to your effort of staying alive. Here are some sources of carbohydrate:

SUGAR MAPLE TREE: Gather the liquid coming out of an accidental or purposed wound site of these trees.

SYCAMORE TREE: These are not as rich as sugar maples but still contain carbohydrate.

GREENBRIER: Remove the thorns and chew on the stems to get a slightly sugary taste, which will include sucrose.

BERRIES: Aggregate berries (those that have numerous drupelet particles) are edible. Other berries vary widely to their edible or toxic nature. A hard, dedicated study must be engaged in before you can make sound decisions under the stress of survival. Some good choices are blackberries, raspberries and strawberries.

FRUITS: Wild fruits include persimmons, pawpaws and wild grapes.

STARCH-LADEN PLANTS: These include cattail roots and plantain.

CHICORY: There are three complex sugars in this plant. Eat the blooms and make a tea with the roots.

PROTEIN: Protein is what helps you continue to have the muscle mass needed to do work. There are several ways to get protein in a survival situation:

NUTS: Most nut species will need to be leeched of their tannins before they are palatable. If water is available, boil them in several changes of water before consuming. Acorns, beechnuts, pecans (these are very regional) and hickory nuts are great choices for protein.

SEED FRUITS: Seeds from seed fruits are much smaller and sometimes require a fair amount of effort to harvest. They include maples, foxtail and wild sunflower. Many seeds that you will find in larger fruit, such as grapes and persimmons, are either toxic or simply not worth the effort of harvesting.

VITAMINS AND MINERALS: For short-term survival, these are probably the least important in the scheme of things. I mention them simply because if your bodily systems are stressed due to the situation it certainly helps to get some vitamins when they are available. You otherwise risk becoming sick and more weakened. Good sources of vitamins and minerals include the following:

PURSLANE: This is absolutely one of the most nutritious plants on the planet. You need to identify this plant and practice finding it so you are prepared if you need it. It contains vitamins A, C and E, as well as various B-complex vitamins, antioxidants and omega-3 fatty acids.

CHICKWEED: This plant contains fats and carbohydrate along with vitamins A, B1, B2, B6 and niacin.

PINE NEEDLES: A very large dose of vitamin C can be had by making pine needle tea.

NATURE'S GROCERY AND HARDWARE STORE: CATTAILS

If, in a survival situation, you find yourself around cattails, consider yourself winning the survival jackpot. Every portion of this plant is useful in some way.

RHIZOME: The roots are rich in starch and carbohydrate. Mash them in water and drink the liquid that comes off. Bring the mixture to a boil to avoid contaminants in the water.

YOUNG SHOOTS: These are edible as they are.

STEMS: Stems can be used to make a hand drill.

LEAVES: After maturing, leaves can be used for bedding and mats and, when they are woven, can be made into shelter, hats and baskets.

YOUNG (GREEN) HEADS: These can be eaten like corn on the cob.

MATURE (BROWN) HEADS: These can be used for fire-starting tinder and insulation in clothes or bedding.

POLLEN: Early in the season, pollen can be gathered and put into soup or broth and consumed.

GRASSES: All grasses are edible and contain various amounts of nutrition across varieties. They do contain a large amount of fiber, so our recommendation is to put the grass in your mouth and chew on it, swallow the juices, then spit out the remaining grass. Getting large doses of fiber in a survival-related event is not a situation you want to be in.

EDIBLE INSECTS

Unfortunately, the United States has determined that eating insects is a "gross" thing to consider. All the while, people from all over the world regularly eat them and enjoy doing so. It is highly recommended that you avoid brightly colored species as these will often be toxic. I also avoid black ones as they are sometimes toxic as well. This is done to avoid the problems that occur from poor decision making during survival. Here are a few options for edible insects:

GRASSHOPPERS AND CRICKETS: You must first tear off the wings and legs as they will often get hung up in your throat when you try to swallow them, even if you chew them up well. Do not eat them raw—skewer them with a stick and cook them on a hot rock or boil them for several minutes. Eating a solid handful or two of them will give you plenty of protein without the need for the hard digestion process.

GRUBS, LARVAE AND WORMS: These can easily be found around rotting logs, stumps or trees. Avoid the black and red ones as there are toxic species in those colors. The others you can place in boiling water and then eat after a few minutes of cooking. Earthworms are full of earth, hence the name. Simply starve them for a day, or squeeze the earth out by hand before eating.

ANTS: Ants are most inactive in the early morning hours. At that time, you can open an ant's nest and get out the egg sacks. To do so, simply disrupt the nest to get the ants moving. These nests are simply loose sand or dirt, and they are easy to disrupt with your shoe or a stick. Place them in boiling water or cook them on a hot rock. Adult ants can also be eaten, as many contain vitamin C. I avoid eating too many as the formic acid in them will often lead to headaches, which aren't worth it, particularly since ants are not rich in other nutrients.

LET TRAPPING WORK FOR YOU WHILE YOU DO OTHER THINGS

As you can see, your approach to obtaining survival food sources should be multifaceted. Trapping is a better choice for obtaining meat sources, because it provides you the opportunity to let the traps work for you throughout your time in the wilderness, while you can stay in a shelter and maintain warmth and energy. Much like hunting, which I will discuss next, you must put in the time to practice trapping before you need the skills. You can also place as many traps as you have materials for. This means you can be in multiple places at once when attempting to get game.

When you start going after animals, you need to understand some of the generalities that will help you get them. Nearly all small-game furbearers are edible, including squirrels, rabbits, mice, raccoons, opossums, foxes and many more. All birds are edible. Please also note that you should follow all the hunting and trapping laws in your respective area.

There are three main parts to any trap. In layman's terms, those are:

1. the engine (the portion that makes it go);

2. the trigger (the portion that holds the trap in place until an animal releases it); and

3. the grabber (the portion that grabs the animal and either kills it or holds it in place until you can get to it).

There are hundreds of traps and trap configurations. I am going to look at two primary classifications and one of each that are efficient and easy to set up.

The stick leading to where the rocks meet is the trigger, when it is moved the top rock will fall on the animal.

2. Place the ground stick in such a way that it pivots on the rock stick. Please be sure the stick does not go deeply into the earth. You can do this by placing a rock or similar hard surface under the base of the stick in the ground.

3. This pivot point is created by cutting a notch in the rock stick and carving the end to match it on the earth stick.

4. Similarly, notch a horizontal stick that matches the end of the rock stick as well as the earth stick.

5. Attach the attractant or bait to the horizontal stick.

6. When the animal goes after the attractant, it will trigger the mechanism in such way that it falls and crushes the animal.

DEADFALLS

Deadfalls are traps that use gravity to drop a heavy object onto an animal. This object can either crush, and hopefully kill, the animal, or the object can be placed on top of a box or similar design of sticks to livetrap the animal. The figure-four deadfall is the easiest to create and can be done with natural materials easily. It also does not require cordage to be utilized. Resources are limited in these types of events; if you can use materials from your surroundings to create the trap, I recommend it.

Creating a figure-four deadfall is easy if you use these six steps (please also reference the image above):

1. Find a heavy rock or log and rest one end of it on the ground—the other end will be suspended in the air by a vertical stick that pivots on the stick detailed in step 2.

SNARES

Snares are designed to catch an animal, most often with some sort of a noose. The preferred method is to catch an animal around its head so that its neck is either broken or it is asphyxiated. This is typically done by throwing the animal into the air, which is why that sort of snare is referred to as a flip snare. Some traps, by desire or mistake, will sometimes catch an animal by the leg. These are referred to as hold snares. Depending upon the material of which the snare is made, most animals will find a way to get out of a hold snare, even if it means chewing off their own leg to free themselves. This is a great method used by trappers who have the means to carry several pounds of steel traps to and from a location. It is not the best for survival trapping, because you do not have the means to carry the heavier yet more effective traps of this nature.

BAIT AND ATTRACTANTS FOR TRAPPING

FOOD: Know what animal you are trying to catch; use a food source to which they are attracted to bring them in.

URINE AND FECES: Urine and feces of another animals are like business cards in the wild. Animals will investigate them to determine what animal is in the area, what that animal is consuming and so on.

SCENT GLAND: Some animals, such as the beaver, use scent glands to mark territory and attract the opposite sex. If you know how to harvest this from one animal you have trapped, you can then use it to bring in others.

ANIMAL PARTS: Parts of dead animals, particularly organ tissue (since this is survival and you have probably already used all the other parts), will attract animals because they will attempt to discover what killed the animal. Sometimes this can also be a deterrent up close. Therefore, I use this in the general area of a trap but never directly in the setup.

Creating a basic snare is easy using the following five steps (please also reference the image to the right):

1. Find a well-used game trail.

2. Create a noose and place it either vertically or horizontally on the trail. If you place it vertically, you are more likely to catch the animal by the head. If you place it horizontally, you are more likely to catch it by the foot. Use small branched sticks to keep the noose from lying directly on the ground.

3. Tie the trigger mechanism (this could be two broken branches, as pictured) to the noose.

4. Tie the other end of cordage to an engine, such as a tree branch.

5. Place bait in and around the snare.

A training setup with orange paracord. Use a natural color in actual application. Funnel animal to trap with sticks.

Make barbed ends when possible and use gigs for any fish or animal you need to catch without your hands.

HUNTING STRATEGIES

Hunting is not unlike trapping in that you must engage in the practice of it long before you actually need the skill. For survival, you need to consider it from two different levels: primitive and modern. You need to learn primitive methods because you may be caught in a situation unexpectedly and have no hunting gear. If you do have the ability to take specific gear with you, there are a few pieces that I recommend, which we will discuss shortly.

PRIMITIVE HUNTING: A great piece of advice given to me by a primitive-skill teacher of mine many years ago was to always consider how the native people of any given area went about supplying their needs. In so doing, you will in essence have the knowledge of where to apply skills to meet your needs if you are caught without any gear. Rocks, "rabbit sticks" and gigs are three tools that I can see being useful to you if you are in this position:

ROCKS AND SLINGS: David used it on Goliath—you can use it on a small-game animal. Most slings require some sort of cordage to be more primitively made, such as dogbane, hickory bark or milkweed. I feel this is a possibility in modern times because you can tear a shirt to form cordage or use laces from your boots to form an effective sling.

"RABBIT STICKS": These are sticks that are about the length from your elbow to the middle of your hand. They are usually a larger diameter than your thumb but smaller than your wrist. Despite the title, these throwing sticks can be used on any small game, including small birds. The intended use is to throw it at an animal and either kill it or momentarily stun or injure it enough to go to it and dispatch it.

GIGS AND SPEARS: These can be used to pierce an animal or press it to the ground for further dispatch. Forming a gig is easy if you follow these five steps:

1. Choose a branch or tree that is about 2 inches (5 cm) in diameter and the length is the same distance from the ground to your armpit.

2. Tie one end off about 6 inches (15 cm) down. This prevents it splitting during the next step.

3. Split the stick in quarters from the end down to the cordage you tied it with.

4. Sharpen each quarter to either a barbed gig point or spear point.

5. Harden the end in a fire.

MODERN HUNTING: This is where you have packed appropriate gear and use it to hunt animals in a situation where you are lost and do not have the ability to self-rescue:

BOWS: There are any number of bows available for your use in hunting situations. In this particular text, I want to consider tools that are purposed specifically for survival. This assumes you have packed this equipment and do not necessarily intend on using it unless an emergency arises. A good example of this is the Survival Archery Systems Tactical Survival Bow. This bow system contains breakdown arrows that fit into the riser of the bow along with the string, making it the only bow of its kind to be self-contained.

GUNS: There are hundreds of options here. For survival methodology, I believe that a .22 long rifle is the best all-around choice. It can take down small game and large game with well-placed shots to the medulla oblongata. It is also incredibly easy to carry many rounds of .22 long rifle ammo without too much weight. There are a number of rifles that breakdown for this purpose. Some good choices are the Ruger 10/22, Henry AR-7 and Marlin 70PSS. You can also get a .22 long rifle pistol that is much smaller and easier to carry (but you sacrifice accuracy due to shorter barrel length).

THE BASICS OF TRAPPING AND HUNTING ANY ANIMAL

I have mentioned more than once that you must practice and prepare before you need these skills. First, I recommend you obtain the appropriate trapping and hunting license for the area in which you want to hunt. You can find hunt clubs or contact the natural resources office of your state to find out how to get started hunting. These fine folks will help you get started on your way.

Second, recognize that game animals are no different than you in that they need shelter, water and food. If you are hunting a specific animal, then get an understanding of how they go about obtaining these resources. This will help you place yourself in the right place to see more game (e.g., near a water source). You cannot simply go into a wilderness indiscriminately and come upon wild game.

Third, know how to mask yourself in the wilderness. Scent is a big trigger for animals. If they smell you, they will often leave or go to a place of safety, such as a den area. Camouflaging is also important. To properly camo yourself, move from shadow to shadow in the wilderness and put as much vegetation as you can between you and possible game trails—just enough for you to shoot through and at the same time mask your movement. Movement is key to game animals. If you move in such a way that they can see you, they will run.

A fishing kit should be lightweight, affordable and easy to assemble in the wild.

FISHING

Fish are like other animals in that they have places they find security in, and they prey on smaller animals and insects for their food. When utilizing any of the following methods for fish, go after them in those areas:

LINE AND HOOKS: These items are so small and lightweight, every survival kit should include some amount of them. You can use sticks or punk wood as a bobber so you can suspend bait in an area known to harbor fish.

NETS: Forming a primitive net is nearly impossible due to resource management for most; however, paracords, tarps, shirts or garbage bags can become impromptu nets. If you are with others, get downstream of them and have them walk to you kicking up rocks and overturning material in a creek that you can walk in. Fish, crayfish and other edible aquatic species will come downstream and into your net.

GIGS: The same tool I discussed on page 115 can be used to gig fish, frogs and snakes.

PROCESSING GAME

Processing game is fairly simple. When doing so, be aware that the fur of mammals and the digestive system of all game (including fish) are the only portions that could potentially be harmful to you. Many birds carry mites and insects, as do some furbearers. The digestive tract contains harmful acids and bacteria, so avoid puncturing them and do not eat them in the wild.

The steps for processing four-legged animals are as follows:

1. If you hunt or trap an animal and do not kill it upon first contact, then do so by striking it with a stick on the base of the skull where it meets the spine. Do this from a distance. Do not grab it with your other hand first.

2. Cut the animal's carotid artery and throat region and gather the blood if possible. Boiling the blood with some water and drinking it will provide you with needed carbohydrate.

3. Cut around the animal's anal opening to detach the anal tract from the skin.

4. Chop off the animal's feet at the ankles.

5. Cut the skin on the hind legs from the ankle to the anus.

6. Start pulling the hide off from the animal much like you would a sock.

7. Once you get the skin off to the neck, cut off the head and neck. Remove the eyeballs and put them in some water to boil and eat. They contain valuable vitamins, minerals and water.

8. Lay the animal on its back and pull the inner skin layers and muscle tissue up and away from the abdominal area. Cut a small slit in these layers, making sure you do not cut deep into the organ tissue. Once the small opening is made, you can more easily see the organ tissue and avoid it to completely open the abdominal cavity with a cut from the ribs down to the anus.

9. Your next goal here is to get all the way to the esophagus and cut it, then make your way to the anal tract. Carefully pull it through the pelvic area.

10. Once the esophagus and anal tract are cut, carefully pull the organs out of the body. Look at the organ tissue. See if you can see any major discoloration on any portion, especially the liver. Look for white spots. If you find these, discard the organs. (Remember, you can use them as bait).

11. Boil water and wash your hands before you use them to place food in your mouth.

12. Please note you can eat the heart, lungs, kidneys and liver. Each of these provide plenty of nourishment (especially the liver, which contains many vitamins and minerals).

13. Boil the bones in a container with water and suck the marrow out of them. They have ample amounts of nutrition. This should be done first so you can get energy without overworking a starving digestive tract.

14. Cut the meat into manageable pieces and cook them over the fire with a stick or on a hot rock.

STORING MEAT

COLD STORAGE: If you are able, place meat in a plastic bag and place the bag in cold running water, such as a river or stream. There are cases where Alaskan hunters stored meat in this manner for 30 days or more.

COOL STORAGE: Cover meat with large, nontoxic plants (such as large leaves). Dig a hole in the ground, until the earth or rock you are digging feels cool or cold. Place the covered meat in the ground and cover it with earth and rocks. It should keep for approximately two days.

SMOKING AND DRY CURING: If plenty of firewood is available, cut meat into very thin slices and build a "grill" from green woody stems. Let the heat from the fire not cook the meat but dry and smoke cure it. Be sure to check that the meat is evenly done through the entire thickness of the meat.

SPOILAGE TESTING: Before eating any suspect meat, recognize that your biggest danger is bacteria. The first indicator that bacteria is active is a pungent smell to the meat. Not all spoilage will be indicated by smell, however. Note if the meat you are considering has been at temperatures above 40°F (4°C) for over an hour. If so, it is very possible to have harmful bacteria without any odor. This is a risk that is not worth taking in a survival situation.

PROCESSING A BIRD

1. Cut the head of the bird off—there is not enough nutrients there to warrant the calorie expenditure of processing it.

2. Cut off the lower legs and feet that are exposed without feathers covering them.

3. Feel near the bottom of the breast toward the legs. You will feel the breast come to a point.

4. If you feel on the anus side of the point, the tissue will seem softer and without muscle structure—that is the abdominal cavity. It will be your entry point to remove entrails.

5. On smaller birds, you can pull it apart with your fingers. On larger birds (e.g., ducks, turkeys), you often need to make a small slit.

6. Once inside the body cavity, run your fingers on the rib-cage side of the cavity to near the neck.

7. Hook your finger and begin pulling the entrails out.

8. Some entrails may linger near the anus. The lower colon is rather easy to pull out without getting feces on the meat.

9. You can pluck the bird to get to the skin. Although this process is very time-consuming, it is worth the calories and fat you will get from the skin.

10. If you are not in a position to pluck a bird, you can begin to peel the skin (along with the feathers) away from the breast. Remove and discard the skin and feathers.

11. Thoroughly clean your hands with whatever is available. While all birds are edible, their plumage is notorious for holding insects and bacteria.

12. Put the meat in a pot to boil or cook it over fire. Gather the cooked juices whenever possible. Break the bones and eat the marrow for calories.

PROCESSING A FISH

1. If the fish has skin, cut around its head, then pull the skin off like a sock. If it has scales, use the edge of your knife to scrape them off. Scraping the scales in the opposite direction they lay is the best method for this.

2. Remove the eyeballs and boil them for consumption.

3. Cut off the head and set it aside to use later for bait on land for mammals and in the water for turtles.

4. Run your finger on the inside of the body cavity along the spine. Once in the rear portion of the fish, "rake" your finger toward the opening to remove the organs.

5. Place the fish on a stick or hot rock to cook it. Be sure to chew the bones up considerably well. The marrow has incredible nutritional value.

PROCESSING A SNAKE

1. Kill a snake utilizing the Trimble method, which is to use a thin branch from a distance and "whip" the snake directly behind the head. You know the snake is dying once it starts to coil up on itself and roll to its back. Never try to pick up any snake with nothing more than your hands.

2. You can also trap the snake by the head with a stout stick.

3. Cut off the head about 2–3 inches (5–8 cm) behind the point where it intersects the body. This will ensure you do not get in the venom sacs, which are located in the head.

4. Peel the skin away from the body like removing a sock.

5. Slit the body on the underside along its length.

6. Remove the organ tissue.

7. Place the meat on a stick or hot rock to cook.

8. Similar to fish, you can eat the snake's bones—just ensure that you chew them well.

SECTION III

TACTICS

The word tactics has, in modern times, been most often utilized in regard to military or naval operations of some sort. While this definition is certainly one that is appropriate, tactics is also defined as "any mode or procedure for gaining advantage or success." Therein lies my use in our purposes here. Having skills is one thing, but putting them to use is a whole other matter. The goal in wilderness survival is to do anything you can to gain an advantage. Sometimes this does involve the use of firearms as a means of gaining an advantage over a stronger or more skilled aggressor. Other times this might mean developing your kids at a young age to be self-reliant and skilled survivalists. This offers you an advantage for you and your family (or any other group) simply because you have more numbers of skilled survivalists. You may have noticed a common thread thus far. Virtually everything I have written has been from the basis of understanding that you are alone and without help or assistance. How advantageous would it be if you had three more people with skills just like your own? It would be a huge advantage. In this section, I am going to discuss the ways of solid leadership and how to develop the ability to work with others.

CHAPTER 11

THE REALITIES OF GOING SOLO AND GROUP FORMATIONS

ALONE WE CAN DO SO LITTLE, TOGETHER WE CAN DO SO MUCH.

—HELEN KELLER

Skiing is a wonderful activity for families and thrill seekers who enjoy the rush of a controlled descent at high rates of speed.

It was just such a rush that a nineteen-year-old woman was seeking in the winter of 2009 at a California resort. What exactly happened to this young lady will never be known. The temperature was in the 20s Fahrenheit (in the negative Celsius) with a slight breeze. There was poor visibility due to falling snow.

This young lady had just started her day of skiing on that cold February day. Around 10 a.m., she skied down the hill and was separated from the party she was skiing with. Some friends and acquaintances had skied down before; others skied down after she had. After not seeing her at or near the bottom, it was assumed that she had gone skiing on another route. Slightly more than six hours later, she was reported missing at 4:40 p.m. A hasty search was put together by SAR personnel. She was found at 5:30 p.m., which was less than an hour since she had been reported missing.

She was found only a few feet from the ski runs, but was under approximately 16 inches (40 cm) of snow. She was declared dead at 7 p.m.

You will undoubtedly note that from the time this young lady was lost until she was found was approximately seven hours. The time between when she was *reported* missing until she was found was fifty minutes. In the weather conditions experienced that day, you would be uncomfortable but alive if you were on your own for fifty minutes. It is those hours between when she went missing and when she was reported missing that cost her her life.

If you ever come in contact with someone with military training, they can easily tell you about their "battle buddy." In the military, your battle buddy is the person who goes to the shower when you shower, goes to the bunks when you go to bed, goes to the latrine when you take a poo. I think you get the idea. They go everywhere with you. This is done for safety. From the military perspective, it is too easy to get lost, kidnapped or injured when no one else is around.

I am going to borrow that mind-set for this scenario here. The young lady in our tragic story went off alone with no accountability to where she was going. No specific person expected her at any time in particular. She then lost her way and no one was aware she was gone. If she had a "skiing buddy" that buddy would have known she was gone when she did not show up at the bottom of that run. In that situation, that person could have immediately notified SAR personnel.

When she was discovered, she only had a thin top on and no boots. There was no apparent trauma. The coroner determined that she had died of hypothermia.

Since she was only a few feet from where others had skied throughout the day, it is evident that she was hard to see. Since she took off her jacket and boots at some point, we can assume she was conscious at the time she got lost. Therefore, she could have also easily used a safety whistle to bring attention to herself. She also could have placed some colorful bandana, portion of jacket or similar item on the outside of a tree she was stranded under to bring attention to that spot.

Had she made herself more visible or blown a whistle, and had the authorities been notified sooner, she would be skiing another day. However, by the nature of her going off alone, she was incapable of making others aware of her location. This event illustrates the importance of being in contact with others for adventurous fun or in a survival-related event. In that regard, I want to focus our attention on how to best work with others.

REALITIES OF GOING SOLO

There were many explorers like Daniel Boone, Simon Kenton, Simon Girty and Lewis Wetzel (not to mention the dozens of unaccounted for Native Americans) that went into wilderness settings and lived solo for many months at a time. Please let me break some hard-to-hear news to you: you are not Daniel Boone.

This seems to be lost on many in the reenacting, survival and prepping movements. One of the questions I ask new students at the beginning of my wilderness safety and survival classes is, "How many nights have you slept in a wilderness setting on the ground in the last year?" I will get answers ranging from zero to dozens of times. If I were to ask the same question of Boone or similar counterparts he would say, "Over three hundred." For that day and time, there was a rougher and tougher breed of man. Nearly all had endured hardship to simply stay alive.

Very few in the modern world, particularly in America, live with that much day-to-day stress and hardship. That is what forced these men to do what they did. We know who they are because they were extraordinary. Even those who surrounded these men could often not imagine themselves doing such exploits. I say that because for those who have a large number of modern conveniences, it is going to be hard to do it at all. To purposely do it alone is near madness. It has been my sincere hope that by relating these real-life scenarios to you that reality has, and will continue, to set in for you. To go it alone is hard, very hard. To do so you will need to:

➡ build a semipermanent shelter that will need to be maintained daily;

➡ adapt your body to the climate (this means you will need to simply deal with the temperatures or build a fire to combat them);

➡ develop detailed hygiene plans and have access to clean water; and

➡ already have in place detailed knowledge of edible plants and hunting and trapping strategies for the long-term.

I thought I could do it. I made successful trips for 30 days on two different occasions when I was younger. I took only a knife with me, trying to push the limit of my knowledge and skills. I did this one time during the summer months and did quite well, albeit a bit hungry most of the time. The weather was hospitable and my needs were fairly easily met because of the conditions. I attempted it again during wintertime. Even in the semi-easy conditions of a Kentucky winter, I had an incredibly difficult time staying out more than three weeks. I nearly starved to death during that particular adventure. I tell you this from experience. Going solo is incredibly hard—harder than you can imagine. Do not choose to do it unless it is your only choice.

LEADERSHIP, GROUP PRINCIPLES AND UNDERSTANDING DEVELOPMENT PHASES

Groups form in various ways. Some are put together at a workplace to accomplish a project. Others are formed by marriage and geographic location. Still others are formed out of necessity. For whatever reason your group has formed, there are stages to group development in any situation.

As a challenge course facilitator and contractor for the Department of Defense, I have assisted various groups ranging from special forces operators and ROTC cadets to sorority girls and homemakers to better form their groups. If you understand the basics of group formation, you too can take an inefficient, unproductive group of people and make them more capable in a very short period of time. The key is to know who the leaders are—those leaders actively working the group toward the same end. I will first consider how to recognize or develop a leader and then discuss the stages of developing the group.

LEADERSHIP QUALITIES

The United States military is one of the best institutions on the planet at developing leaders. One of the aspects of leadership development that assists this process is the institution of rank and hierarchy. Without it, and the unquestioning duty of those beneath a leader, they would fail. While this can be a model for one to consider, it is quite different for those who find themselves in a survival situation without a known, stated-as-such leader.

That is why you should be developing yourself—whether it be at home, work or play—into an effective leader. By so doing you will recognize when someone else exhibits leadership qualities that surpass your own and you can then support that person in your mutual endeavor of staying alive. There are five qualities a good leader should possess:

MINIMAL EGO: A good leader should be confident and not cocky. Cockiness leads to false bravado under stress. Time and time again, survival situations have proven to break those who are cocky.

INTEGRITY: Most recognize from our own places of work that if a boss or supervisor is not consistent with judgements and ethics, then it will simply demoralize others in the workplace. A good leader must be able to admit when they and others are wrong and have the communication skills necessary to see opportunities for improvement.

GOOD COMMUNICATION SKILLS: An effective leader will have the ability to converse and be direct when it is needed and soft when that is needed. The basics of good communication skills are born out of having good awareness skills. Being aware of subtle body language and what it indicates is important. With good communication skills, a leader will be inspiring for others. Please also know that good communication skills also include good listening skills, not simply talking skills.

TEAMWORK SKILLS: Nobody likes a dictator. Make sure that the person who is leading a group is willing to "get their hands dirty," not simply standing back and watching people do it.

DECISIVENESS: Being ambiguous is not a good quality for a leader. A leader must be the type that gathers as much information as possible. Some situations allow this to happen over several hours, and in other situations you may only get seconds. Either way, take as much information as possible and make a decision.

GROUP AND LEADERSHIP PRINCIPLES

Once a leader is determined organically or systematically, that leader (or leaders) and the group must work together. Working together is at the heart of what I teach as challenge course facilitator. In that "laboratory" environment, almost always outside, one can easily see breakdowns in the group, which can be addressed and worked through after the teams leave. After several years of studying, guiding and facilitating groups focused on leadership development, I have put together five basic principles of quality groups and their leaders that are high-functioning:

WHAT THE HECK IS RLTW?

In short, it means *Rangers Lead the Way*. It is an acronym you will often see and hear if you are in the company of some Army Rangers, which I have been on a number of occasions. I have never been a Ranger, so I do not use the phrase. However, these fine men that endure the hard, dedicated training of both Ranger school and assignment to the Ranger battalions oftentimes are the spearpoint of military operations. Their use of the RLTW motto shows the significance of how important their work is. As an outside observer, I consider Rangers the epitome of these leadership skills being utilized.

1. WHEN WORKING WITH OTHERS, KEEP FOCUS ON THE SITUATION AND NOT ON THE INDIVIDUAL PEOPLE INVOLVED. The goal of survival is to survive. In most situations, someone has made a mistake that put them in that place. I am certain you have discovered this on your own by reading all the various scenarios at the start of each chapter. For the group, especially the leader, to allow anyone to focus on the person responsible will only further hurt the situation. You must focus on the tasks at hand. That does not mean that the error is not addressed. It must be, so everyone knows what to do in the future. By focusing attention on the person, you demoralize part of the group who could be a loved one of the responsible party or someone who is useful to further the survival of the group in the future.

2. MAINTAIN THE SELF-CONFIDENCE OF OTHERS. Each person in a group is going to need some assistance at some point. That is when I like to offer them some PCP. No, it is not what you are thinking. Praise, correction, praise is what I am talking about in this regard. Remember, this is not the military I am talking about, where everyone is required to take orders from those above. Where this official hierarchy is not in place, you will need to ensure others continue to be productive. Here is how I handle a situation where someone needs to be corrected: I will be supportive by telling them something they are doing well (praise), correct the inappropriate action or behavior (correction) and then offer them support to get back on it and get to work at the end (praise). An example would be, "I appreciate that you have a desire to gather some firewood; however, you must make sure to not pick wood off the ground because it almost always holds moisture there. Now that you know that, go pick up some more because you are certainly going to need it." See what I did there? Praise, correction, praise.

3. **MAINTAIN CONSTRUCTIVE RELATIONSHIPS.** Do not allow someone to socially disengage from the group. In true survival, you are going to need everyone you can get to accomplish things. Some will want to disengage and not be involved, which is step one in the "giving up" process. This is a problem not only for that individual person but it will also serve to bring the group down if you have someone disengaged. Work diligently to keep everyone engaged.

4. **TAKE THE INITIATIVE TO MAKE THINGS BETTER.** If there is a problem or an issue, then set the example by taking care of it. Do not wait until "someone else" takes care of it.

5. **LEAD BY EXAMPLE.** This builds upon all the principles but puts it more succinctly. You must lead by doing. Sometimes that means you must lead others to relax and breathe (see Chapters 1–5). You need to be the example of the behavior that you want the group to emulate. If they see you as anxious and afraid, they will be anxious and afraid. As a leader of any group, be the person you want them to be.

GROUP DEVELOPMENT STAGES

You should be able to look at your group and recognize where they are in the process of becoming a working unit. It was psychologist Bruce Tuckman who, in 1965, developed this model for helping to develop groups in any environment. This could include corporate, military or sports teams. This process works very well when it comes to developing a survival group:

STAGE 1: FORMING: Due to this being very early in the process, most people in the group will be polite, courteous, positive and all will make some effort to make things work. During this stage, it is the leader's responsibility to be dominant. You will need to set standards of acceptance as well as roles for those in the group.

STAGE 2: STORMING: In this stage, those in the group will begin to push boundaries and personality conflicts will occur. People will start to focus on their individual goals rather than their team's goals. People will start to jockey for position or resources in an effort to take care of only themselves. This is where most groups, particularly those in survival situations, start to dissolve and fall away to failure. As a leader during this stage, you will need to make sure that everyone has roles and that everyone knows it is a team effort. The others will need to see the benefit of working together.

STAGE 3: NORMING: Once differences are resolved, the group will begin to see how they build upon one another's strengths. Socialization will become more natural and the members of the group will start receiving constructive feedback from one another. The people will start to blend into their respective roles, but at the same time skills will overlap and there will be duplication of effort. It will be the leader's responsibility to make the work more efficient and remove the overlap. A redistribution of skills will almost always be necessary at this stage.

STAGE 4: PERFORMING: At this point, the group is functioning as a proper unit, rather than individuals. It is easy to be part of the team. However, due to the nature of it being a survival situation, the stresses that come with hunger, injury and more may cause the group to dissolve (sometimes only partially). It is the leader's responsibility to bring the group back to proper and efficient action.

These are the basics of group formation and their leaders. There are so many variables to a true survival situation that everyone must remain fluid and ready to roll with the punches. Change is inevitable in this type of situation, and a well-functioning group with proper leadership will be able to meet these inevitable hardships with strength to overcome them.

It is worthy for me to discuss how a group would handle a situation in which you are hiking, mountaineering or hunting in a wilderness setting and for some reason find that your entire group is now in a position that you must stay in that setting. Reasons could range from the simple (e.g., you got lost) to the more extreme (e.g., there was a landslide and your exit road was washed away or otherwise covered in water). Whatever the reason, take this knowledge of group formation and utilize it for your advantage. Here is a listing of how to go about doing exactly that:

DETERMINE A LEADER: This is not necessarily the person with the most woods experience but rather the person with the most leadership experience. Use knowledge of proper leadership to ascertain who the leader should be. I force my students to do this (under stress) in basic wilderness survival classes. Oftentimes what happens is the group chooses someone who is in need of some positive reinforcement. I allow this to happen so the group can watch itself fall apart. This is not a time for you to build someone up and create a leader. A leader will either naturally stand out, or the group will intellectually determine who it should be based on knowledge of one another.

DELEGATE TASKS: This is the beauty of a group setting. Remember the Rule of Three and how you have to order things due to time constraints and priorities? With a group, you can assign someone the various tasks that need to be completed. I would suggest that the group first build a shelter together that will hold everyone. The time constraint for it is only a few short hours depending upon the climate. However, it is easy to have one group gathering this type of material and another group gathering other materials so that tasks are not duplicated to an extreme. Once a shelter is built, the group can be further subdivided to accomplish fire-, water- and food-related tasks.

STAY TOGETHER: Remember the notion of having a "battle buddy" from earlier in the chapter. This is never more important than in a scenario of this nature. It is very easy for one person to wander off while gathering materials and get lost. This compounds the problem. If you do not have enough people to have "survival buddies," then you must keep a visual on a central point. If you are going to leave the visual area, you must inform the leader of the direction you are going and agree to not travel excessively far.

PLAY GAMES: Think of this situation in the same way you do long road trips that get boring. To keep your mind active, you can play games. Something as simple as tic-tac-toe with rocks or scribbling with sticks in the dirt will help to keep the mood light.

As I have suggested, ask questions of one another to get good information when making a plan on how to survive. At no time should you allow one person to "play hero" and leave the group. There are too many accounts (two listed in this book) in which that person died and the others lived. Work with the statistics—do not let them go.

CHAPTER 12

SHELTER IN PLACE OR BUG OUT?

IT IS NOT THE MOUNTAINS WE CONQUER, IT IS OURSELVES.
—SIR EDMUND HILLARY

In November 2006, a family of four—a husband, wife and their two young daughters—left their Thanksgiving vacation and headed toward their home in San Francisco, California, by car. After leaving Portland, Oregon, they determined they would travel toward a resort.

Shortly after leaving, they made a turn near the outer limits of the rugged Wild Rogue Wilderness. It is not known for certain if this change in plans was made on purpose or by mistake. In either case, they eventually got stuck in drifted snow.

This problem arose after they had had verbal warnings from local people, posted warning signs along the roadway and noted warnings on the map they were following.

It is there that the family stayed for seven days. They had stayed warm by running the vehicle until it ran out of gas. They then used some nearby dry firewood to light a fire. Eventually, they burned tires as a means of trying to signal helicopters they thought they heard in the area.

Seven days into the situation, the husband left the car to go get help. He made an estimate that he was only 4–5 miles (6–8 km) from the nearest town. In fact, he was nearly 15 miles (24 km) from the nearest town.

Nine days into the ordeal, SAR helicopters discovered the car. The SAR personnel were able to drop supplies to the mother and the two small girls. Shortly thereafter, another helicopter was able to land and take them to safety. It was only then that the mother was made aware that her husband had never made it to the town.

His body was found later, nearly 12 miles (19 km) from the location. He had died from hypothermia due to his exposure to the elements.

I am using this story this late in the book simply because there are a number of various things this family could have done to help prevent this tragedy. I will list them here but would like to start with the topic of this chapter:

- Stay put, sit down, stop. Whatever you want to attribute the S in STOPA to, just do it. Although I can empathize with this father, his wife and daughters lived through this situation because they stayed with their shelter, which was the car.

- They did not follow the critical Rule of Three or any basic, commonsense approach to travel. They had clear and distinct warnings to not travel the area they got lost in. They ignored them all.

- They did not know how to read a map. The map they had was accurate and the scale was correct. They assessed the area in which they found themselves to be only 4–5 miles (6–8 km) from the nearest town. They were very far off in their estimate.

- Their clothing choices were poor. When the father left the area to get help, he had tennis shoes and a light jacket; he took some bright clothing with him to mark his trail.

- They ate some food while they were there, but ignored their water intake. Eating without hydrating properly would have used up even more water stores in their body. They were surrounded by snow and at one point had a fire. This combination should have supplied them with usable clean water by the gallons. With a car they could have improvised any number of pieces of it to fashion a makeshift container.

- They did not have basic car-kit supplies. They had travel clothes and gear for vacation, but no preparations for the event of an emergency. No one knows when these emergencies will happen. You need to prepare a car kit now and put it in your vehicle.

- It is so simple but needs to be emphasized here: they should have notified someone of where they were going and when they expected to return. This family could have easily been rescued in plenty of time and without much issue. The authorities were not notified until the father did not show up for work on time. It only took two days for the proper authorities to be mobilized after being notified from staff at his work place in San Francisco. It was around that same time that the father had set out on his fateful trek. He would have never made that decision had the authorities been notified sooner.

➡ Ego definitely got in the way here. The father tried to save the day. Many have done the same. It is noble but foolhardy just the same. It is known that he backtracked on the road for several miles and then tried to take a shortcut down a ravine. After so much hard work and stress, it is certain that his decision-making ability was hampered greatly.

Without a doubt, one of the most idealistic methods of survival and preparedness training is the concept of "bugging out." Bugging out is the notion of grabbing a vehicle and or backpack and heading into the wilderness to make a temporary or new long-term existence for yourself. This notion is far from being realistic for the vast majority of those who hold it so dear.

In the story, I considered a surprise lost-in-the-woods event. Even for those that are more prepared and purposely put themselves there, the reality is that living in that environment long-term is stressful at best and downright foolhardy if based in reality.

WHEN BUGGING OUT IS REALISTIC

One of the students in a class I taught several years ago was a mere 20 miles (32 km) from the Chernobyl nuclear plant when it experienced the explosions and subsequent meltdowns in April 1986. She literally had to grab her two children and what supplies she could place in her arms and go in the opposite direction. She eventually crossed a river by floating on a log with her children and those few supplies. She found herself on an island, which gave her the isolation she needed to stay safe from the rioting that followed. At that time, many women who were alone were physically assaulted, raped and left for dead. She eventually left the island and gained refugee status in the United States, where she became an American citizen. She remarked to me that since that day, she has never gone anywhere without a go bag of basic supplies. I say that to recognize that there certainly are times when bugging out might be the best solution. Let's consider some realistic possibilities for just such a scenario.

SHORT-TERM BUGGING OUT (LESS THAN A MONTH)

Natural disasters (such as hurricanes, tornados and earthquakes) and man-made disasters (such as nuclear meltdowns, biological threats and terrorism) are reasons that a short-term bugging out scenario can be an effective method to keep you and those you care about safe. This would include finding relative safety and shelter as soon as possible. It should also include the ability to keep yourself away from others. In large-scale disasters, people begin to act like animals in a few hours. Therefore, you must remove yourself or be able to provide your own safety.

LONG-TERM BUGGING OUT (MORE THAN A MONTH)

The only situation in which I feel that long-term bugging out is a good solution is when you already have a distinct plan to leave and a location to go to. This location should be able to provide adequate first aid, hygiene, shelter, water and food supplies. These can either be stored or acquired in the area. The idea of living in a tarp setup with what you can carry on your back is not realistic.

However, as I have suggested, it might be your only option. For example, what if there was an earthquake in an area where the infrastructure was not designed to withstand it? There would be massive destruction and chaos. You have two choices at that point: join the multitudes of others who will rely on government assistance programs or make it on your own. During Hurricane Katrina, regular citizens became animal-like in their actions. I would go so far to say that this is natural. It is much like fight or flight. When you and others, rather unexpectedly, are fighting for the same limited resources, it can be life threatening. By removing yourself on a long-term time frame, you can avoid those issues that challenge your personal safety. The only people with real-world experience in this regard are those that have lived a homeless lifestyle in which they have had to scavenge and forage for supplies. The lessons from being homeless are ones that cannot be duplicated in a training event very easily.

CONSIDERATIONS FOR BUGGING OUT

In either case, there are a number of considerations that you must go through in the planning stages of this sort of event:

LOCATION: To be prepared for a bugout, you must have supplies with you at all times to make your way to a secondary location. At all times you must have the skills to go in that direction. You should be prepared to physically make it there. Also, you must have a communication plan for those in your family or group to have a rally point to meet before going there. If you do not currently have such a plan, you need one. This includes your children. They need to understand that you are coming for them in the event of a disaster. These events do not happen when everyone is sitting around the house, packs by the door, ready to go.

HEALTH AND WELL-BEING: Do you and the members of your group have the ability to make it to a secondary location? Are there those in the group with special needs, such as diabetes, inability to walk long distances, age considerations or other needs? If so, you need to prepare supplies for their medical needs and transportation strategies if they cannot walk any longer.

PETS: Do you value your pets as if they are part of the family? If so, you will want to take them with you. You will need to supply water and food for them as well. If not, then you will need to deal with the negative morale that will come with leaving them behind.

THREAT ANALYSIS: Take a very long, hard look at the actual threat. Does it indicate only a possible problem or a likely problem? A possible problem needs to be considered and watched carefully. A likely problem must be addressed; if it is not, you will get bogged down in the stress of an event and not make appropriate decisions.

COMPARISON TO HOME: Now, compare these situations to your staying in your home if it is available. If they are normally the same, then the best strategy would be to stay there. If there is a reason that your home is not a reasonable choice (e.g., if it was destroyed by the disaster), then you will need to bug out.

ATTRIBUTES OF A GOOD BUGOUT LOCATION

When determining a good location to bug out, there are a number of things to consider when assessing whether it is a good one:

- Is it in a location that is defendable? If aggressors attempt to overtake it, can you properly stop them? It should have good entrance and exit points if you are overrun.

- It should be camouflaged and not on a regular thoroughfare where others will see it.

- A good water source should be nearby. Even if you have to purify the water before using it. Gathering and cleaning water is much easier than creating it.

- Hygiene supplies are a must-have in this location. There are a number of solid preparedness plans put out by FEMA and other governmental agencies tasked with such planning. Poor hygiene conditions are the number one cause for death in those long-term situations. Many take for granted that there is easy access to water and cleaning agents.

- It should provide appropriate shelter in all seasons. A good thought is it should have a stove for wintertime and the ability to vent heat in the summer.

When determining the bugout location, there are also some important skills and tools that would be most helpful during a long-term event. These are things that are primitive or near-modern in nature. Often referred to as "old skills," these are skills that many people had less than one hundred years ago but very few have today due to modern technology. If that modern technology is no longer available, these skill sets are going to once again become incredibly valuable:

METALLURGY is a near-modern method of developing tools from raw material or discarded materials and is a must-have skill. Blacksmithing is a practice you should engage in to develop tools and practice. Here is a listing of the basics that can get you started:

- You will need a forge, which is a hearty design of metal in which you can place coal, ignite it and give it a steady flow of air to get it excessively hot. When viewing it, the coal should be at or near white-hot to make steel pliable.

- You will need high carbon steel to work with. Some good choices that you can find are railroad spikes, leaf springs and rebar. You certainly want a steel that has rust on it. Stainless steel and those steels with stainless materials in it are not useful for blacksmithing.

- Make sure to have an anvil to pound metal into the shape you need it to be. This can be an actual anvil or any very dense, large, hard piece of steel.

- Hand tools such as files, pliers and similar items to hold material as you form and shape it are essential.

- You will need a good hammer. To shape metal, a good flat surface on one side and a rounded surface on the other is a good choice if you must have only one tool.

- Blacksmithing is part art and part science. Find a blacksmith and invest into training with them. Many will do it for free, others will ask a small fee. It is well worth the investment. Just because it is free does not mean it is not important.

CONTAINER MAKING is developing containers from natural or modern materials. Knowing how to sew with a needle and thread is a valuable skill to fix clothing as well as make bags for containers. Basket making is another primitive skill to invest time and money into. Have buckets on hand and look at your workplace, your car and around your home and places you recreate. What things could you use to hold water or other materials you may want to carry? How can you make a handle to make it easier to do so?

CORDAGE MAKING involves making rope, string and other cordage and is one of the most time-consuming materials to make in a primitive setting. Having plenty of it on hand is essential to long-term usefulness. You must also be aware of your surroundings to see what you can use to make cordage. When I bring this topic up to most

Paracord, jute or dogbane cordage is invaluable to wilderness surviva. Carry some with you and know how to make it from your environment.

novices, the obvious answer of "I will use vines" comes up. Most vines are typically of two kinds: those that are pliable but weak and those that are strong but not pliable. This makes it such that they will not actually be useful in this sort of situation without dedicated practice and study. There are many natural materials that can be used in place of man-made cordage. You will want to braid, wrap or weave it together to make it stronger. Some good choices are cedar rootlets, dogbane, milkweed, hickory bark and animal hair. Some good modern choices to make cordage are discarded clothing pieces, plastic bags, garbage bags and duct tape.

I have focused a lot of attention on shelter location in this chapter. Please do not forget that you will need supplies whenever possible. That is why I detailed that topic in Chapter 7, and I have a detailed listings of gear in Chapter 15. Location is important for personal safety and acquiring resources. If you have the ability to carry some supplies with you each day, you will save valuable time and energy in the all-important early moments of an event.

In the next chapter, I will discuss and consider armed defensive strategies. As I mentioned earlier, the reality is that in true disaster in wildernesses or rural areas, people can become animalistic in a hurry. In our country, we have been fortunate that large-scale warfare (other than the Civil War) or natural disasters have not occurred to put you in a position of large-scale defense with arms. It is my sincere hope that it stays that way. At the same time, I do not want to stick my head in the sand and neglect the obvious answer of self-defense on a larger scale.

CHAPTER 13

PATROLLING AND DEFENSIVE STRATEGIES WITH WEAPONS

IF YOU ARE GOING TO BE A BEAR, BE A GRIZZLY.
—MAHATMA GANDHI

In June 2015, two convicted murderers escaped from a maximum security prison in New York state. It was later discovered that they had had assistance from prison personnel, who gave them power tools and other equipment.

After twenty days of intense searching, law enforcement personnel were informed of a lead nearly 20 miles (32 km) from the prison. A cabin in the area had been broken into. Basic food supplies had been taken along with at least one weapon.

Upon reaching the area, a U.S. Border Patrol team located and shot one of the inmates after he would not put his weapon down. Two days later, the second inmate was found along a road and ran from a New York State Police trooper, a mere 2 miles (3 km) from the Canadian border. The trooper made contact with the inmate and gave him verbal orders to stop and give up. After the inmate made threatening movements toward the trooper, the trooper was forced to shoot the inmate. He was then taken alive into custody.

This story is indicative of what lengths a person will go to avoid imprisonment. Further that situation by knowing that the rule of law is in place, meaning two murderous, dangerous criminals were on the loose, and law enforcement was aggressively seeking to bring them to justice. It is the reason that I am very appreciative of all that law enforcement does. Imagine for a moment, however, a time in which that same rule of law does not exist, one in which lawlessness is not an irregular occurrence but the norm. I am not a fan of conspiracy theories nor am I anti-government. I do believe that large-scale disasters—such as Hurricane Katrina and Hurricane Sandy, the 2004 tsunami disaster in Indonesia and earthquakes all over the world—are indicative of the lawlessness that can occur when large groups of people are quickly taken away from their normal lives.

This particular true story is a small glimpse of the extremes to which those who have no problems breaking the law will go. They will lie, steal, kill and more to stay alive and get to a better life than their current situation. If widespread lawlessness were to occur in our country and the already-stretched resources of law enforcement were pushed to their limits, it would become necessary for families and other groups to work together to defend themselves.

Let me be clear at the onset of this of this discussion: bringing harm to others is not a goal or desire of mine and those that I train with. I am also not advocating anti-government action with arms. It would be our greatest desire to affect change where needed through our words, voting choices and the political process. The likelihood of a need for you to have an armed group of individuals is minimal in a wilderness setting. At the same time, with the chaos that occurs in the world today, I do not want to stick my head in the sand and pretend that danger does not exist. I am therefore going to present this information in an attempt to help you and your family or group to be more self-reliant if such an event were to occur.

Please bear in mind that my knowledge in these areas is education-based and not experienced-based. I have been fortunate to train in armed tactics with wonderful instructors who have decades of experience in military and law enforcement settings. As a student of The Scott-Donelan Tracking School, I had the opportunity to work with officers who tracked both the escaped prisoners in New York and Eric Frein in Pennsylvania. One thing has been made abundantly clear to me in that environment: avoidance is the key to keeping safe, especially when it is a family group rather than a team of seasoned operators. The dynamics that present themselves in that sort of group versus those who have extensive training are numerous. This material is presented in such a way that it can be used by just such a group.

It bears repeating: avoidance should be your focus. When avoidance strategies do not work and you make contact with those who are armed and mean to do you harm, the only answer at that point is to return with a controlled use of force to displace the problem.

As this chapter progresses, please reference the section in the hunting chapter on camouflaging tactics. Those same principles will apply in this as well.

PATROLLING AND MOVEMENT STRATEGIES

If there is a known or likely threat in an area in which you must move about, the goal should be to minimize exposure whenever possible. This means you will most likely want to move at night, if at all possible. There are some considerations to moving at night:

- ➡ Moving at night minimizes the visual exposure to you and your group.

- ➡ Moving at night will require you to have some prior knowledge of the area in which you travel.

- ➡ Moving at night puts you at greater risk if your aggressors have night vision, infrared or thermal imaging technology.

- ➡ Moving at night increases the likelihood of separation from your group or family.

Because of these considerations, the need will arise for you to have scouts who go and gather information and bring it back to the group. This will allow only those scouts to be exposed. Since they are responsible only for themselves, their attention and awareness can be focused on themselves and their objective rather than the activities of the whole group.

When the whole group does need to move together, proper patrolling formation will be key to minimizing the exposure of the group to dangerous areas.

Utilize a herringbone patrol formation with space front to back, and side to side of each person.

BASIC PATROLLING

"Terrain will dictate your tactics" is an oft-said phrase when discussing movement strategies. This is especially true in a wilderness setting. Not only does the land structure pose a problem, but the undergrowth, waterways and more will force your group to move in certain ways. Ideally, you should move about in a herringbone formation with a "bound" between you and the people closest to you. The herringbone formation is one where you stagger a line in such a way that no one is on either side of another. If you were to view the formation from above, it would look like a *Z* pattern traveling back from the lead to the final person in formation. A bound is a tactically appropriate distance between you and the person closest to you. Imagine you are lying on the ground unseen and searched for by a sniper. If you were to jump up, start to run, recognize that the sniper can see you, then drop again out of sight, that is a bound. You will often hear people of a tactical mind-set refer to this on TV and movies as, "I am up, he sees me, I am down."

This tactic gives you distance that, should you be engaged in contact with an aggressive group, you would minimize those that can be shot or otherwise easily seen by one person. Typically, in any patrol formation the person up front is the most likely to make contact. Whoever is in this position should have great observation and awareness skills.

The team leader should be placed somewhere in the midst of the group, sometimes near the end, so as to be able to effectively communicate with others in the group without much sound. Noise and light discipline is of utmost importance. This means you should keep communication to a minimum and very low if speaking person-to-person or on a radio. Movement is the key to being seen in a wilderness setting; therefore your movement should be purposeful and deliberate. If contact is likely to be made, the movement must become more cautious.

PLANNING FOR THE UNEXPECTED

Before a group goes on a patrol, there are a number of things that should be determined. This will give the patrol group purpose and efficiency so that it minimizes risk. Please bear in mind this is different than a military setting, where a patrol may be tasked to go and find an enemy. They often have support, even if it may be days later. For the patrol formation in a survival situation within a wilderness setting of a nonmilitary group or family, support is not likely. Things to consider are:

- ➡ the intended destination of the patrol;

- ➡ the time frame to complete the patrol;

- ➡ the purpose of going out;

- ➡ the rally point, as well as secondary and tertiary contingencies should the group become disconnected; and

- ➡ land-navigation skills for group members so you can communicate about areas without seeing them.

When discussing details, such as a map, always maintain security for the group.

In this manner, there are stated purposes and everyone in the group knows what they are expected to do. Please know that if contact is made and rounds are going in various directions, the ability to communicate will degrade to near zero. Highly trained operators spend countless hours of training to overcome this problem. That does not mean you should not practice these methods. I study and practice these methods in the tactical survival course that I co-teach with Iron Sight Defense. Practice what you read in these pages, take a class when possible and definitely get together with your group to run through drills.

SETTING UP A CAMP WHILE ON PATROL

People are not machines and they will have to rest. Simply stopping and everyone taking a nap or sleeping overnight is not acceptable in this type of situation. You will need to set up a secure camp. If this is done properly, those in your group will get adequate rest while the others keep a secure watch as a means of protection.

While on patrol, the land navigators should use terrain analysis on the map to determine possible sites to set up the camp. This will save the time and effort of going to locations first. Once that is completed, the patrol will send out scouts to survey and recon the area to see if it is actually an acceptable location. Once they determine that it is and they return to the group, the entire group will then patrol to the area.

When choosing a site to set up a camp, ensure that it has the following qualities:

DEFENSIBLE: If another party finds you, can you make an adequate defense of your position and remove yourself from it?

CAMOUFLAGED: This does not mean you necessarily have to have camouflage surrounding it and over it. It does mean that you should choose a spot and equipment that blends well with the surroundings. If you are moving about in camo and then you pull out a red sleeping bag and use it, you are not camouflaged.

ACCESS TO CONCEALMENT AND COVER: Concealment is that which will assist in breaking up a person's outline and the gear; however, bullets can fire through it. Cover is earth or similar barriers that will serve to stop bullets. This is only temporary as cover will eventually be eaten away. If contact is made, you will want cover nearby.

Natural or man-made indentations in the earth provide a more secure and hidden sleeping position.

NOT LOCATED ON A HILLTOP: Being on a hilltop makes it easy for movement to be spotted due to the silhouette with the skyline.

Once the patrol has made it to the location, the group will effectively be split into two distinct groups. One group will provide security. The other group will start setting up their sleeping positions. Once they set up their positions, they will then go and relieve a person providing security so they can do the same.

SLEEPING POSITIONS

Sleeping positions should be such that you are a bound apart. You should also be able to make visual contact with those on either side of you at least and everyone in the group, if possible.

Setting up the camp is a process where, until everything is completed, no one is done working. Particularly when people are tired, dehydrated and hungry, they will often go into self-preservation mode. Once they get their sleep position set up, they are ready to stop and take a break. This defeats the positive aspects of the team, and team leaders should be on the lookout for this behavior. It will take a team effort to accomplish these tasks.

Here are the basics of the camp setup:

➡ Sleeping positions should be dug in to give a smaller profile as well as a shooting position with cover if needed.

➡ An outer ring that is cleared of forest debris should be created on the outside perimeter of the camp. This will allow security to patrol the area at night while making minimal noise. If there are inexperienced members of the group, you may want to ring it with cordage in the trees. This will provide a reference point in the dark so no light is needed. It will also serve as an early warning system for those that might infiltrate the perimeter. You can attach any number of noise makers to the line to facilitate this.

➡ An inner ring should be cleared of forest debris that connect the sleeping positions of the members of the group. This will allow members to make contact with other members without waking the entire group during the process.

➡ The amount of security through the night will be determined by the number in your group. At a bare minimum, you should have two people providing security through the night. They will walk the outside perimeter, slowly and deliberately, stopping often to listen for noise out of the ordinary. A good rule of thumb is for security to take a step every 30–60 seconds. Two security personnel will be opposite of one another on the perimeter through the night.

➡ Security and sleep should be done in shifts. This also greatly depends upon the number in your group. If possible, have security up and at it for two hours on, six hours off. This assumes you have a group of eight members. If that number is smaller, then divide it equally of four hours on security, four hours in sleep. If you have more than this number, more people should be able to provide security, meaning you will then have four people moving about the perimeter.

➡ If a fire is needed for warmth, boiling of water or cooking, dig a hole and build the fire in the hole. Also, build it close to a tree. The smoke will travel up the tree and then be spread into the forest canopy. This will lessen the ability of others to determine where it is coming from. By keeping the fire small and in a hole, it will help keep light discipline.

Crossing a danger zone will require protection from the team.

CROSSING DANGER ZONES

While on patrol, there will come a need for the group to cross an area in which the likelihood of being seen and targeted is greater. This is an incredibly vulnerable place to be and should be avoided when possible. Some examples would be crossing a road or open field or going to the edge of a waterway to get water. You can consider the open area as the place where bullets will travel, so you should minimize your time in that location and provide security for those traveling through it. The steps to do this follow:

➡ Notify the patrol that you need to cross a danger area.

➡ Two security personnel will come to the edge and find cover.

➡ You can imagine that these two security personnel are the edges of a door and that everyone else will go through the door.

➡ They will then provide security in opposite directions from one another looking down the edge of the danger area.

➡ Everyone else in the patrol will quickly move through the "door" to the other side of the danger area. This will be done with a bound between each person.

➡ Once everyone is through, two new security personnel will set up to provide security on the opposite side of the danger area from where they started.

➡ Once they do, the original security personnel will cross the danger area with a bound between them.

MAKING CONTACT WITH ARMED AGGRESSORS

Making contact comes in two forms: offensive and defensive. Defensive contact is typically made when your group has been ambushed or otherwise surprised. Your actions are therefore reactive rather than preemptive. Not reacting in a gunfight is a terrible answer; reacting to contact is secondary in terms of your being successful. The best position to be in is offensive when possible. This puts you in the driver's seat and makes the other party the one who must react to the contact. I would like to emphasize again that this should only be done when you know for certain that the lives in your group are soon to be threatened (i.e., a confrontation is going to occur and is unavoidable).

There are many methods for making contact, and they require extensive training in learning how to shoot, move and communicate. If your group has that sort of training, you will accomplish much with even a small team. If, however, your team is small and does not have that sort of training, things will need to stay simple so you can accomplish your self-defense. I recommend for such teams the use of the *L* formation for when contact is made. For the sake of our discussion, I will assume you have a four-person team and contact is made on the patrol's right:

➡ If you are in an ambush position for offensive purposes, you will have two people (Team A) that begin the firefight as a group moves through or is encamped.

➡ The other two in your group (Team B) will be at a 90-degree angle to Team A. Once the enemy is engaged, they will most likely find positions to address the rounds coming at them.

➡ Team B should be in position when that occurs to finish the job.

➡ Team A will then push forward to clear the area.

➡ Team B will follow behind them on their line to ensure that the area is secure.

I have mentioned observation and awareness skills throughout this book. They are the hallmarks of everything ranging from completely keeping you out of danger to knowing how to see more things around you under heavy amounts of stress. Tracking is the ultimate in having good observation and awareness skills. In the next chapter, I am going to teach you the fundamentals of tracking and show you some ways to use it for wilderness safety and survival situations.

CHAPTER 14

TRACKING: THE ULTIMATE IN OBSERVATION AND AWARENESS

NO DOUBT TO YOU IT APPEARED A MERE TRAMPLING LINE OF SLUSH, BUT TO MY TRAINED EYES EVERY MARK UPON ITS SURFACE HAD A MEANING.

—SHERLOCK HOLMES

In many parts of Appalachia, there is an epidemic of sorts caused by the cheap drug trade that surrounds methamphetamine production. Due to its toxicity, ease of production and relatively low cost, many impoverished people utilize it as an escape from the realities of life: jobs, family and stress. Many in this area therefore choose to steal from others to afford to buy the drug.

On one farm in central Kentucky, near the heart of this drug plague, a couple found themselves face-to-face with a thief stealing an ATV, chainsaws and copper wire to pawn. Since the thief came by them at a high rate of speed, he was gone from sight before the gravity of what was occurring came to the minds of the couple.

The husband gave his wife a sidearm and told her to go into the woods and hide until he returned. He then set off to find the thief and hopefully retrieve the property. He tracked the four-wheeler for approximately 300 yards (274 m) through the farm, following displaced leaves and water splashes through puddles. Sometime later, he came upon the thief a mere 10 yards (9 m) away, stuck in heavy brush after he wrecked the ATV. The thief stepped toward him with a small hammer in a threatening manner. After a direct conversation, the thief left without the gear and the husband called the proper authorities. After doing so, he began to track the individual, but after 219 feet (200 m), lost his tracks and other signs in an area where there was little to no brush or leaf litter on the ground. While getting in a comfortable and safe overwatch position, he waited and watched. He then heard a deer snort and dogs barking on an opposite hillside. He gained a better vantage point and could then see the thief running down an embankment. It is there that he directed law enforcement to the thief's direction of travel so they could begin a search and possible arrest of the individual.

The husband then went back to the area in which he asked his wife to go hide. He then tracked her to her hiding location so that she could safely come out.

I am not encouraging the average person to take fugitive apprehension into their own hands. The husband in this story was a trained tracker in the ways and methods of military and law enforcement tracking.

This story indicates how, in a matter of mere seconds, a simple day out in even a small wilderness can become a deadly situation. The husband of this story was able to employ tracking as a means to get all of the equipment back as well as lead law enforcement to the thief.

This story does not detail a deep backcountry experience. It does detail a wilderness setting and how one could simply read the ground in a timely fashion and under much stress to help resolve a problem. Let me help you get started on learning how to read the signs to inform you of what is or has been going on around you.

BEING "TRACK AND SIGN AWARE"

The idea of self-rescue is a situation in which other methods of taking care of your needs have failed. The statistics and research support our notion that the best method for you to increase the likelihood that you will survive an event is to stay in a safe place, meet your needs and wait until help arrives. I think I have also proven to you that the best method to overcome a survival situation is to not be in it in the first place. That is why I have covered so many topics in-depth under the auspices of safety. These are all meant to keep you from danger. One of the most overlooked aspects of wilderness travel is the ability to track and use that ability to keep you (or get you) out of danger.

Hollywood and those with a desire for ill-gotten gain would have you believe that tracking is some magical, otherworldly skill set. It is not. Tracking is nothing more than having good observation and awareness skills. It does require an ample amount of time to become a good tracker. It does not take that much time to develop the ability to be "track and sign aware" so that you can see where you and where others have been, as well as avoid dangerous animals. I want to consider these two aspects of tracking—sign and tracks—in such a way that you too can assist yourself. I will also offer you direct suggestions on how you can utilize tracking in survival situations.

WHAT IS SIGN?

Sign is nothing more than a change in the normal state of an environment. I refer to this as disturbance as well. This is anything that makes the baseline of what you are looking at appear different. There are three broad classifications of sign that I will consider: ground sign, aerial sign and intangible sign.

GROUND SIGN is anything that happens at or below the level of the average person's ankle. This includes tracks, about which I will go into great detail later. Some instances of ground sign are the following:

> **BROKEN VEGETATION:** If a person or animal steps onto dead or dying vegetation, it will break. If a person steps onto fragile or delicate vegetation, it will also break.

> **BRUISED VEGETATION:** Vegetation that is heartier does not necessarily break. It will often have bruising on it when it comes under pressure and is squeezed. For example, let's assume you step on grass but there is a rock under it. Where your foot squeezes the grass between your foot and the rock, there will often be bruising.

TRANSFER: This is particles of ground medium that adheres to the bottom of a foot or shoe and then comes off later. If you were to walk from a beach onto a cement sidewalk, some of that sand will carry onto the sidewalk. Understanding that makes it easy to see if someone leaves a trail of dirt or sand in leaf litter. They will carry some of that with them and vice versa. This can also include water splashes from creeks, rivers, ponds, puddles and so on.

IMPRESSIONS: If there is a stick, rock or similar object that lies directly on strata that is less dense than itself, when the denser material is stepped upon, it will leave an impression in that strata.

DISPLACEMENT: Much like transfer, displacement is the movement of particles on the ground, but they are not necessarily moved due to adhering to the bottom of the shoe or foot. Some examples would be a stick or rock that has been kicked forward, scuff marks in moss, leaves overturned, leaves creased or bark pulled off of downed logs.

Verify aerial sign with ground sign. Note the broken branch and overturned leaves in the second photo.

Disturbed leaves, overturned moss, bruised and/or broken vegetation are examples of ground spoor.

AERIAL SIGN is any change from the baseline that occurs above the ankle. Aerial sign is often missed when one is seeking signs and clues in an effort to closely view sign on the ground. Tracking requires you to look down, up and all around in an effort to take in as many clues as possible.

BROKEN BRANCHES: Broken branches are an indicator that something has passed a certain direction. This gives you an indicator of the height of what you are searching for. Breaking branches is something that you may have seen in the movies as a means of indicating a trail. Lost people will sometimes do this if they need to leave sign.

Note that you see the bottom of leaves and the white of the freshly broken branch.

SKINNED BARK: Skinned bark will happen when something comes in contact with it that puts direct pressure on it. Bark in large amounts rarely falls from a healthy tree due to gravity. Do not bypass the branches of an area in favor of just looking at tree trunks. It is the branches that people will more likely make contact with than a trunk.

COBWEBS: Cobwebs that are missing indicate something displaced them. Cobwebs that are present indicate something did not displace them. Therefore, if you are seeing them, the quarry you are after is most likely not in the area.

MOISTURE ON LEAVES: If a person or animal is walking through an area that is wet from rain or dew, they will inadvertently knock the water off the vegetation.

VEGETATION "POINTERS": When a person or animal walks through tall vegetation such as grass, the grass stems will become intertwined and point in the direction the person or animal walked.

INTANGIBLE SIGN is an amalgamation of sign that I like to separate from ground and aerial sign simply because it may or may not be direct displacement of material from an area.

EXCREMENT AND URINE: All good animal trackers will spend time studying the various excrement of animals. It indicates that certain animals are in the area, and can tell you what items exist in that animal's diet. This is an important aspect to consider when setting up proper traps in the wilderness. For humans, you can also get details of the quarry you are tracking. If the urine is incredibly foul smelling it may indicate the person is dehydrated and looking for water. If you are tuned to the smell of excrement and urine you may catch the odor in the wind and be able to follow it.

GARBAGE: This could include bottles, clothing, portions of food, spit or tobacco products. These are obviously placed there by humans and their presence can indicate the passage of time from when they were placed and then found.

ANIMAL SOUNDS: Most animals, especially birds, have feeding sounds, mating sounds and alarm sounds. If you are in search of someone, they may alarm an animal that then makes that sound. Some examples are deer snorting, squirrels barking and birds alarming. If you cannot see the person, the alarm sounds could indicate a person is in that area.

The key to seeing more tracks is to constantly ask yourself WHY you see the tracks you do see.

WHAT ARE TRACKS?

A set of tracks, or an individual track, is simply an impression from a person or animal left on the ground. There are many reasons the track itself is visible. Light and shadow play an important role in what you actually see in a track. In this regard, I tell my students that the order of things is "sun-track-you." What I mean by this is that you should always place the track between you and the sun when viewing it. This also means that if you are searching an area that you think contains a track, again, place that area between you and the sun. The reason for this is simple. When the sun casts light onto the track, it also casts shadows inside of the track due to the edges of tread, the outline and so on. Most trackers will tell you that the best time of day to track is early in the morning or late in the evening. This is certainly true for those that track in arid environments, because there are not that many natural barriers that cause light displacement in those locations. For those in a wilderness setting, light is displaced due to trees, canopy, bush vegetation and more.

SEE A TRACK

OUTLINE: The outer limits and perimeter of an individual track. The ideal full track rarely happens in the real world unless the strata is conducive for it, such as sand or mud.

VALUE: The visible lightness or darkness of a color. For example, a leaf has one value when it is dry, but is typically much darker when it is wet.

SHAPE: Human tracks are the only ones in nature that have sharp 90-degree angles within them. Lugs, the outer edge, heel box and toe box often have lugs that are made so that they dig into the earth to propel you forward. These portions will have unique shapes that do not appear in nature. Animals have distinctive characteristics. Look at the shape of the individual parts as well as the outline shape.

TEXTURE: When baseline is rough, a track will smooth it out. When baseline is smooth, tracks will roughen it up.

COLOR: Color changes are those that have been caused by passage of a person or animal. Dark mud on a dry leaf, blood on the ground, overturned leaves or flowers displaced from a stem are all examples of how color will be normal in one place and be out of the ordinary in another.

RHYTHM: This is normally seen as gait patterns in humans and other animals. Steps have a certain rhythm to them that do not just randomly appear in nature.

Therefore, utilizing a flashlight to serve as a small stand-in for the sun is wise counsel. Using a flashlight, you can force the light onto the track in the place that you want it and can therefore force the shadows as well. This will negate the need to use the sun as the only light source for your tracking needs.

Track aging is most definitely the part of tracking that gets a high volume of preconceived ideas in modern movies and TV. My thinking is that you can determine if something is relatively old, relatively new or of unknown age. Rob Speiden of Natural Awareness Tracking School was the first to put that in observable language for me when I studied tracking with him. I have come to greatly appreciate that understanding.

Note the fading edges and less distinct pattern on the old track on the left vs. the distinct visible tread and water splashes of the new track.

RELATIVELY NEW: Not all of these attributes will be indicated in a new track, but each of them are possible indicators of one—there are sharp angles in the track itself; minor tread patterns can be seen; moisture is present; few materials from the area have fallen into the track; and there are natural materials pressed deep into tread marks.

RELATIVELY OLD: The lug and outer edges are broken down; the track indicates moisture similar to the strata surrounding it; leaves or other debris in the track have started to come out of it; surrounding debris have started to fill in on top of the track; and other tracks are on top of it.

UNKNOWN AGE: Do not discredit this notion. In our discussion of decision making earlier, I noted how you can get bogged down in details and not get things accomplished. This is never truer than with track aging. As a training method, you can never study it enough. As a useful method, if you spend too much time discerning age, you are then spending valuable time on that issue when you could be determining other information.

HOW TO USE TRACKING FOR SURVIVAL

This information may seem a bit misplaced for a survival book. Much like the focus on mind-set in the first five chapters, I believe if you study tracking you will keep yourself out of most troubling situations. I have fabricated the following scenarios so that I can discuss how to use tracking in them.

SCENARIO 1: You are part of a small group that is going overnight hiking in a large wilderness area with lots of marked and unmarked trails. Your group stops to fill up water containers as one of the group leaders continues up the trail to scout it out and set up camp. After you fill up and make the bend, the trail splits in two and you had not communicated with your group leader beforehand on which side he would take.

USE OF TRACKING: You should be able to notice on the trails where there is relatively new ground sign. At a fork, a person will make a turning of their foot on the ground to change direction. This will show up as displaced ground particles, overturned leaves or more.

SCENARIO 2: You leave a well-marked trail to view the area from an interesting overlook and to pick berries for food. Once these activities are completed, you then want to make your way back to the trail.

USE OF TRACKING: On your way to the area, leave "sympathy sign" or "courtesy clues." This is the process of purposely disturbing the leaf litter, breaking a few small branches or even leaving man-made material on the trail to pick up on your way back out. If your tracking skills are good, you do not need to leave a lot of this sign. If they are not so good, leave a lot of sign.

SCENARIO 3: You go on a camping trip and have a large group. This large group will have need to dig a latrine since you will be staying in one central backcountry camping spot for several days. The latrine will need to be far away from camp.

USE OF TRACKING: This is an easy way for others to get lost on their way to or from the latrine. You can leave sympathy sign. Another good choice is to leave a chem light or similar light source at the latrine to make it easy to find in the dark. Not hard-core tracking, mind you, but it is intangible sign to help indicate an area to which you need to travel.

SCENARIO 4: You get lost on a deep backcountry hiking trip. You know animals are in the area.

USE OF TRACKING: If you have need to develop trapping or hunting tools, you can determine the travel lanes of various small game by tracking. You therefore increase the likelihood you will catch something. You could also note that you are in an area where you find bear tracks. Alongside of them you note there are small ones as well. This indicates a mother and cubs. This is an area to avoid because animals will defend their young aggressively. You can therefore use your tracking skill to preemptively remove yourself from a possible situation before it occurs.

HOW TO BECOME MORE TRACK AWARE

Training in the ways of a tracker is enjoyable and can be done anywhere in the world. I like to refer to tracking as either being on the micro or macro level. In *micro tracking*, you are picking apart each and every detail you possibly can. This includes looking at one individual track. This is not hard to do on a sandy beach or track pit designed for this purpose. It gets much more difficult when you apply it to a wilderness setting with leaves or forest debris. A good way to do this is to dissect one individual track piece by piece. Here is an example of how to do it:

➡ Purposely step in an area and make a solid, full-foot impression on the leaf litter or forest debris. This should be done in an area you are likely to be in.

➡ Take a picture of the spot. Note the direction of travel with a compass.

➡ Take measurements of what you can see. Look for overall length, toe-box width and length and heel-box width and length.

➡ Sketch the area and any portion of the track that may be visible in the strata.

➡ Pull each and every piece of forest debris from the track. Start with what is on top and make your way to the ground. Make notes on what you observe with each individual piece (e.g., leaves are creased, a pine needle is bent, moisture on the bottom of leaves).

➡ Once you get to the ground, note anything you can about the impression on the ground (if there is one).

➡ Sketch the ground impression if there is one.

With the ten-step drill, one person leaves markers for his training partner to then look at each one and find the disturbance in each.

This will help you start to see these details at a distance. Once you dedicate much time and practice to this, you can then start to see them regularly on your hikes and other treks.

Macro tracking is the practice of taking what you have learned in micro tracking and applying it. The goal would be to understand the terrain and make educated guesses on direction of travel. To be able to do that, you need to practice. This is a great partner exercise and can be done with other students of tracking as well as with uninterested parties. It is done as follows and is referred to as the ten-step drill:

1. Find an area that is similar to the area you may want to track in.

2. Have a defined starting point for one partner.

3. Have that partner take ten distinct steps from the starting point. They will then turn around and either stand or sit down at the end of the ten steps.

4. The tracker then observes the area and finds each of the ten steps and marks them with a small stick, pebble, flag or other item.

5. Once this is done, the roles are reversed and done as many times as you like.

I teach this method because it gives the beginning tracker solid starting and ending points to consider. Once each of the steps is determined and marked, you can then see the overall picture and direction of travel. This serves to help observe the overall situation and how tracks will affect a landscape. To continue this practice and to improve your skill set, you must begin to make it harder and harder for the tracker. When you start having trouble observing tracks, remove some of the difficulty barriers and start again. Some examples would be:

➡ giving an ending point, but not a starting point;

➡ giving a starting point but adding more steps so the quarry is not seen by the tracker; and

➡ purposely walking through various strata that changes (pine needles, leaf litter, sand, mud, dirt, grass, thick brush and other environmental changes all track differently; change it up).

Work with a team to determine the tracks. Getting feedback is essential to seeing what others are seeing and developing new ways of seeing tracks.

Now that I have laid the foundation of knowledge without utilizing much gear, it is time to consider how various gear pieces play a role in your survival. Keep in mind that statistics prove that having a strong mind-set is the key to survival under stress. Do not be dependent upon gear alone to take care of you. In the modern world, it is not wise to forgo the use of gear.

SECTION IV

GEAR

If you reduce humans down as a species of animal, one thing that sets us apart is that we are tool users. We like utilizing tools to complete tasks. I am not referring to just hammers, scales and the like. I am also referring to forks, phones, cars, chairs and more. We like to use things to make us more comfortable and productive. There is nothing wrong with this; it has made us an advanced species in many ways. For survival needs, the problem arises when we become so dependent upon these tools that we forget the basics of meeting our needs without them. If you develop your mind-set, skills and tactics as you've learned in this book, then adding in appropriate gear where it is useful will do two very distinct things. The first is that the appropriate gear will help you stay *out* of many survival situations. For example, you know how to use your map and compass, so you do not get lost in the first place. Second, making tools, shelters and fire in a wilderness setting without modern tools is work. Fun work and good work, for certain, in training. In a true survival setting, it is most helpful to have gear pieces that make survival easier and more likely. Guard your dependency on gear, though. If you become completely dependent upon getting fire by using a lighter, you are setting yourself up for disaster. Also keep in mind that you need to train with your gear so you are familiar with it. I wish I had kept track of the people who have broken knives during survival training with me. Had they not engaged in training, they would have broken it when they needed it. In summary, get some good gear and train with it regularly.

CHAPTER 15

GEAR SELECTION AND METHODS OF CARRY

SURVIVAL PACKING: AN EXTENDED FORM OF HIKING IN WHICH PEOPLE CARRY DOUBLE THE AMOUNT OF GEAR THEY NEED FOR HALF THE DISTANCE THEY PLANNED TO GO, IN TWICE THE TIME IT SHOULD TAKE.

—ANONYMOUS

Lovingly referred to as the "land of many arches" by many, the Red River Gorge Geological Area (RRG) in east-central Kentucky is a haven for climbers, backpackers, day hikers and history buffs from all over the world. Just a quick look at the cars and license plates on the trailheads will quickly tell you that people from all walks of life are attracted to this area, and for good reason. The RRG is home to some of the most gorgeous rock formations and forested vistas on the planet, including the many natural rock arches throughout the area.

The RRG is a unique area of roughly 29,000 acres that is a small part of the Daniel Boone National Forest, which encompasses 2.1 million acres as a whole. This larger area also contains its own natural beauty consisting of mixed hardwood forests and waterways and is teeming with wildlife.

That is exactly what brought four inexperienced and ill-equipped hikers into the RRG for a short day hike in May 2015. The four young men chose a random trail they thought was a loop that came back to the trailhead. They took no provisions—no maps, no overnight gear, no flashlights and evidently no knowledge of the area. Rather than getting on a trail that simply looped back around, they actually stepped on to the Sheltowee Trace, a trail 307 miles (494 km) running the span of the Daniel Boone National Forest. Around 11 p.m., after stumbling through the dark for two hours, the four men decided to call 911. Fortunately for them, they were able to get through.

Due to the wonders of Internet apps, local SAR teams were able to ping their location, get the coordinates and let them know they were on the way. At 2 a.m., the SAR teams made contact with the hikers and escorted them back to their vehicles.

Let's take a look at this real-world scenario and see what mistakes were made and how they can be fixed. The hikers made two very poor decisions:

1. They did no research before going on their hike to see if what they thought was a simple loop trail was the actual trail they were getting on.

2. They took absolutely no supplies with them as they went into the wilderness.

It seems obvious but is worth repeating that basic supplies are a must *whenever* and *wherever* you go out. In our real-world scenario, the young men were incredibly fortunate they were able to obtain cell service to make a call. Had they not been able to make the call, they would have been forced to stay out for the night. A few simple supplies would have taken care of their needs easily. For this particular situation, the following would have been a must for a simple, fun day on the trail:

➡ Land-navigation tools, such as a map, compass and GPS (and the knowledge to use them).

➡ A poncho or tarp for shelter. Something as simple as a garbage bag you can use for shelter is much better than no shelter at all. Building shelter from natural materials is always an option, but it takes a lot of time and energy to build an adequate one.

➡ Water or the means to procure some in the wild using a device, such as a purifying straw.

Each of these combined would have weighed less than 2 pounds (900 g) and could have easily fit into a cargo pocket or small day pack. With that said, that would be a minimalist approach to this scenario. Let's dig into the topic of gear selection and how to carry it.

When it comes to gear, I like to consider the topic from the perspective of tiers of gear, with each tier building upon the first. There are certain pieces of gear you should carry with you every day. There are others that you can stage at various places to keep it ready and useful.

TIER 1: EVERYDAY CARRY (EDC)

This is one of, if not the most, debated and discussed points of survival and disaster preparedness. My view on the topic is simple. Your EDC should be the items that you need to take care of your personal safety. Everyone's personal safety is different, and that is why this topic is so hotly contested. I am okay with a family who lives hundreds of miles from nowhere in Idaho carrying something different than someone who lives in a large metropolitan city. They have incredibly different lives due to geography, weather and proximity to other people. Here are the basic items that are needed to live comfortably on a day-to-day basis:

Everyday-Carry (EDC) items are those you should carry on you each and every day.

IDENTIFICATION AND MONEY: Your wallet and purse need to stay near or on you at all times. This allows you to identify yourself when you can or be identified if you are incapable of doing so (e.g., if you are unconscious). Credit or debit cards are nice and handy to use; however, I believe cash is an important option you must have on you. I always have enough cash in my pocket to get back home from any place I find myself.

COMMUNICATIONS: Being able to effectively communicate with those in your family or preparedness group is important. This can easily be done with a cell phone or ham radio.

TRAVEL TOOLS: That is a fancy way of saying your car keys. You need them to be able to get home or to get away from danger—they need to be close to you or on you at all times.

EDGED TOOL: A knife is an indispensable tool. With knowledge and training, you can accomplish many important tasks with a good knife.

FLASHLIGHT: A small light attached to your key ring is a good choice, but a nice tactical flashlight is a better one. Both can be used in low- or no-light conditions to leave a situation or find the items you need to help preserve your personal safety. A tactical flashlight can assist you in self-defense situations as well. That brings up our next consideration.

SELF-DEFENSE TOOL: This could be the knife. A firearm (and the training on how to use it safely and properly) is a force multiplier when it comes to your safety. Please adhere to all firearm-related laws.

MEDICAL SUPPLIES: These are important particularly for those who are dependent upon such things as insulin or an EpiPen, but they are also essential for all of us. A tourniquet and HALO® Chest Seal are a couple of the basic items you should have access to. Make sure to get training on how to do basic first aid and refer to the first aid section of this book (pages 47–54).

Get first aid training and keep a kit(s) close at hand wherever you go.

LIGHTER: Maintenance of your core body temperature is imperative. A lighter goes a long way in helping you develop a fire to do exactly that.

CORDAGE: A solid paracord bracelet will go a long way to supply you with cordage that is hard to make in the wild.

HOW TO CARRY IT: These are all items that you should comfortably carry on you each and every day. It is not possible to carry some of these items in some jobs and professions. In that case, you should put this gear in a small case, fanny pack or similar holder. You should then have it readily available nearby.

TIER 2: GET-HOME CARRY

What this gear provides is your get-home carry, also known as your bug-out bag (BOB). These are the items that you do not want to carry on your body at all times as you do your EDC. However, they do go out the door with you every day, or you have duplicate items in both your vehicle and home that are easy to carry. I refer to this as get-home carry simply because getting back home in most instances is the best strategy for disaster needs. If for some reason your home or travel corridor is not an option, get-home carry should be able to accommodate your needs as a BOB as well. Get-home carry gear is generally understood to be those materials that you need to survive for 72 hours or less.

You should have Get-Home gear that will help you survive in the event you cannot make it home for a night or two.

Tier 2 gear should expand upon your needs and start to make you more comfortable. The items you need in this level should start to meet your needs beyond personal safety (refer to Rule of Three in Chapter 1). Considering that this gear is for a short-term situation, you will not need excessive amounts of gear. A good goal would be under 20 pounds (9 kg) for this gear, which is an amount that most anyone can carry and that you can carry when you may be injured or otherwise unable to carry heavy weight. That amount of gear can also be easily carried in an inconspicuous pack or bag so that you do not bring unwanted attention to it.

The following are types of needs along with gear suggestions and considerations for each:

PERSONAL SAFETY NEEDS

- 4 x 4-inch (10 x 10-cm) gauze and duct tape, which are much more useful than adhesive strip bandages that fall off

- H&H brand bandages and/or rolled gauze

- Over-the-counter medications, such as ibuprofen, antihistamines and analgesics

- A chest decompression needle and nasopharyngeal airway (see photo on page 158)

- Iodine or hand sanitizer

- Maps to get home from wherever you are

- A fixed-blade knife

- A bandana

- Sturdy gloves

COLD-WEATHER NEEDS

- Extra ignition sources (such as a ferro rod or weatherproof lighter)

- Fuel sources that are small and weigh little (such as packaged fuel cubes)

- Shelter-building supplies (such as a garbage bag, reflective blanket and tarp)

- Weather-appropriate clothing, including rain gear and sturdy hiking or walking shoes

HOT-WEATHER NEEDS

- Clothing and head covering options that will ventilate extra heat as well as keep you from the sun's rays

HYDRATION NEEDS

- Stainless steel water bottles carrying a minimum of 30 ounces (887 ml) of clean water per person

- Personal water filtration device (see Chapter 9)

- Knowledge of your area so you can find alternate water sources to use your filtration device to decontaminate water

CALORIC AND ENERGY NEEDS

- Energy bars, gel packs and powders that do not require preparation and that provide a minimum of 1,000 calories per person per day (provided you will not be working and burning calories)

- Noodles for needed carbohydrate (if water is plentiful)

GROUP-COMMUNICATION NEEDS

- A one-way crank radio that has a light, chargers and AM, FM and NOAA capabilities to monitor news activity

- A two-way radio to communicate with others in your group

- A ham radio (this will require a short but easy test to obtain your license)

- An infrared light source to mark your position at night for those that have night vision capability (note that this is incredibly easy to see with night vision goggles)

Communication devices other than cell phones are a must-have item for families or teams.

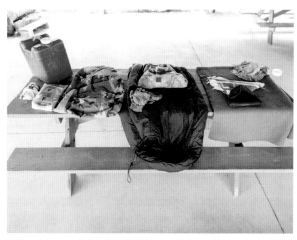

Paracord, jute or dogbane cordage is invaluable to wilderness survival, carry some with you and know how to make it from your environment.

HOW TO CARRY IT: This can vary depending on you and your work and recreation. I carry my Tier 2 gear on a tactical belt and chest pack. It makes it easier for me to do the work I need to do and also allows me to easily carry a backpack for the next tier. You might find it easier to carry Tier 2 gear in an over-shoulder bag or backpack. There are many available options to carry discreetly. Another consideration is to carry in a child's book bag with cartoon characters on it. It does not raise suspicion but also gives you the ability to covertly carry in plain sight. As with all things, carry within the bounds of the law where they are applicable. Tier 2 gear needs to go out the door with you every day and come to work, recreation and back home each day. In this manner, it is always close to you.

TIER 3: SUSTAINMENT CARRY

This is the gear you need for when you are going to have a stay of unknown length. An example of this type of situation would be if you are on vacation when a disaster event occurs. It may take you weeks to get back home. Another example situation would be you leaving on a business trip and a disaster occurs and you want to get back home. Please keep in mind two important aspects when it comes to this gear. The first is that each tier builds upon the others. The second, as discussed in Chapter 12, is that sheltering in place in most situations is your best option. The items here are those that are used only sparingly when you must use them to stay alive. This means keeping an eye out in your environment to meet your needs. When and if you determine your needs are not being met, then you use the items here to meet them:

MRE—MEAL READY TO EAT

Prepare your own MREs with carbohydrate- and nutrient-rich foods, such as rice, beans, granola, nuts, seeds, dried fruits and dried vegetables. Dehydrate and vacuum seal them to suit. This allows you to create what meets your needs and tastes with no need to carry as much weight. More enjoyable food is a huge morale boost.

PERSONAL SAFETY

➡ Camouflage (to hunt game or hide yourself from a human aggressor)

➡ Smoke grenades (to mark a location or to create a diversion so you can leave)

COLD-WEATHER NEEDS

➡ Wool and fleece if conditions are damp or wet; down does not work well when wet (refer to the layers in Chapter 7 for more information)

➡ A sound, packable sleeping bag and bivy sack (such as a solid Gore-Tex® bivy coupled with a liner bivy that reflects heat) or a sleeping bag that insulates (this will add bulk and weight)

➡ Wicking hat and wicking gloves

HOT-WEATHER NEEDS

➡ Sunscreen and a large brimmed hat to keep excess sunlight off

➡ Clothes, such as cotton, that will allow moisture to stay on your body (which serves to cool you down)

HYDRATION NEEDS

➡ Several gallons of water if traveling by car so that you can start a trek hydrated

➡ Hydration pump so you can clean several gallons of water easily

CALORIC AND ENERGY NEEDS

➡ Military-type MREs that are dense and hold enough calories for one day if you are using a lot of energy

HOW TO CARRY IT: Carry this in a backpack for certain, but note that it is going to start getting heavy. I would recommend a backpack that has a waist belt on it as well as adjustable shoulder straps. This way, you will have the ability to carry long and short distances easily.

TIER 4: NEVER-GOING-HOME CARRY

Let me make this clear on the onset of the discussion: I am not a fan of conspiracy theories, zombies and the other concepts that run rampant in the survival and preparedness movement. I think they detract from the realities of what could actually happen in a wilderness or rural setting. Events that could easily cause large-scale disruption in our daily lives are listed here:

ENEMY ATTACK ON OUR SOIL: It is no secret that the United States in particular is despised by its enemies in the world. Many of these enemies would like to see the United States brought to its knees. I am not a military planner or strategist; therefore, I do not see the day-to-day threats that our military, law enforcement and intelligence agencies deal with. I am, however, peers with and train with those who do these things. While they are professionals and do not divulge things of a sensitive nature, they are close enough to advise me that possibilities exist for our nation to be thrust into a large-scale engagement on our own soil.

NATURAL DISASTER: Two possible disasters that come to mind are volcanic eruptions from the Yellowstone area or any number of earthquakes throughout the country. These sorts of disasters are 100-percent guaranteed to happen in the future. When this will happen remains to be seen. It could be five minutes from now. It could be five hundred thousand years from now. In our society, where there is a dependence upon just-in-time inventory measures for food and hygiene supplies, an event such as this would cause far-reaching destruction.

NUCLEAR OR BIOLOGICAL DISASTER: This could occur due to inefficiency of people in our country or could also be the result of an enemy attack. In either case, these could cause widespread disaster that is felt for years.

If any of these events were to occur and you found yourself in a wilderness or rural setting, the things discussed in this text would then become sustainment and living conditions, not simply survival until help arrives.

From my perspective, you will be living your life with a hybrid of gear pieces from the modern era coupled with skills formed during more primitive times. The old adage in survival and bushcraft training, "The more you know, the less you carry," is absolutely true. You should invest time, energy and money into learning old skills and developing gear pieces from your environment

Please remember that not all of these items are even remotely something you could easily carry. These will need to be in your bug-out location or will need to be acquired along the way:

- Long gun for a stand-off weapon that will keep aggressors at a much farther distance

- Ammunition to cover your self-defense, hunting and bartering needs

- Building supplies (a good felling ax, saw and similar tools)

- Bartering supplies (such as tobacco products, alcohol and medical and dental supplies)

- Food to barter (such as chocolate, candy and similar items)

HOW TO CARRY IT: Much like Tier 3, any Tier 4 gear that can be carried here is best for a large, sturdy backpack since it will be a significant load. You can also prep a vehicle for such carry, too. Just be cognizant of a situation where you may have to abandon a vehicle and move on foot. You should train with your gear so you know what you can actually carry.

CHAPTER 16

WEAPONS AND OTHER TOOL CHOICES

I KNOW NOT WITH WHAT WEAPONS WORLD WAR III WILL BE FOUGHT, BUT WORLD WAR IV WILL BE FOUGHT WITH STICKS AND STONES.

—ALBERT EINSTEIN

One fall in the early 1990s, a young lady who had recently been divorced decided to "take a break from it all" and go on a short camping trip with her two small children. Upon arriving in the national forest area, she noticed there was a unique eating establishment for people from all over the world to eat, hang out and trade stories before heading out to hike, bike, camp, climb and otherwise enjoy the beautiful area.

While eating, she was friended by some locals who petted her dog and chatted with her and her children. This was not uncommon as people from all over the world share their experiences and enjoy a wonderful community of like-minded individuals in this central location. After chatting for quite a while, she decided to pack up the kids and the dog and head out to find a camping spot near a creek. She asked her new friends about a possible location since she was new to the area. They gave her several options and let her know the pros and cons of each. Based upon their recommendation, she chose one and headed in that direction.

Shortly after nightfall, she saw approaching headlights along the road she was camped near. She and the children were enjoying a night around the campfire, telling stories and making s'mores. The car stopped near her location and she was happy to see that one of the nice guys from the hangout was simply coming to check on her to make sure she was okay and found everything she needed. She invited him to stay and eat a s'more, which he happily agreed to do.

The young man was a nice addition to the campfire, telling his own fun stories of camping and joining in on campfire songs. It was not long before the children were tired and wanted to go to bed. The mother had a huge family-size tent in which she put the kids to bed and then went back to the campfire to have some adult conversation with her new camp friend. When she opened the tent door to leave it, she was shoved back down into the tent. She was told by her new acquaintance that if she did not make any noise, he would not harm her children. She was then raped, beaten to unconsciousness and left for dead. The new "acquaintance" did not harm the children and left the area.

The most important aspect of this story that I want you to know is that this was an incredibly isolated incident. Situations such as these are statistically very low in the wilderness. However, they do happen and illustrate two points of consideration:

1. Re-read the section on self-defense in Chapter 6. It is important information that should not be overlooked. It includes avoidance and awareness strategies that would have prevented this situation from happening.

2. Owning, training with and carrying your weapon on your person can be a great equalizer against predators. Those predators can be animal or human. In either instance, you need to know what weapons work well for these situations. You must also consider the ones that you can get for your specific needs.

The lady in our story could have easily utilized a weapon to defend herself and her children in this situation. No rational person wants to bring harm to or kill another person. Defending yourself and those you love will sometimes warrant you bringing harm to a predator. In Chapter 13, I discussed the usefulness of various weapons for hunting purposes. In this chapter, I want to look at various weapons you can use for self-defense against predators, human as well as other animal predators.

HANDGUNS

Handguns that are commonly utilized for self-defense come in two basic forms:

The key to self-defense with any handgun is lots of practice and training. Seek out quality instruction.

REVOLVER: This style of gun can typically hold 5–6 rounds of ammunition dependent upon the size of the weapon and the size of the rounds. Revolvers are relatively cumbersome to load without significant amounts of training. When you pull the trigger, only one shot will go off. You will find two types of revolvers: single-action or double-action. The *double* in *double-action* means the trigger performs two functions: cocking and then firing the gun. In a single-action revolver, the hammer can be cocked on its own and the trigger simply allows it to fall. This type of revolver is harder for most people to keep on target when firing multiple times. It does take quite a bit of abuse, even with little maintenance.

SEMIAUTOMATIC: Rounds are held in magazines that you replace when they are empty. These magazines hold various amounts. In the most common calibers, they will hold 6–15 rounds. Again, this depends upon the caliber of the weapon. They are relatively easy to load with little training. When you pull the trigger another round is loaded and it is ready to fire. Various manufacturers' guns, such as Glocks, cycle easily in most shooter's hands. Others may require more maintenance for a novice.

The .22 long rifle is an excellent choice for obtaining game and can also be used for self-defense.

RIFLES

In Chapter 14, I shared with you a story of a tracker who had a direct conversation with a thief, who then fled. That interaction included a rifle being worn by the tracker, which most likely encouraged the thief to leave. The tracker used his skill and rifle to keep a physical assault from occurring.

Ask any qualified tactical shooting instructor and they will tell you that a handgun should be used to defend and fight your way back to your rifle. A rifle for hunting purposes is exponentially more accurate and efficient than is a handgun in the hands of most shooters. This includes those used for hunting as well as self-defense. Let's consider both.

HUNTING PURPOSES

I am a proponent of utilizing the .22 long rifle for survival-hunting purposes. The .22 long rifle allows you to carry hundreds of rounds with little extra weight, is accurate out to the typical small-game hunting distances, can take down large game when shot with precision and is easily packable. I have extensively used three of this type of rifle with much success and will highlight them here for you:

MARLIN 70PSS: This is a breakdown .22 semiautomatic rifle. It has a magazine that carries seven rounds. It comes with an all-weather case that will fit in most day packs and larger.

RUGER 10/22: This is one of my favorite .22 semiautomatic rifles and has proven to be a tack driver. The takedown model easily comes apart and goes together with ease for safe and accurate use.

HENRY AR-7: This model is unique in that it breaks down and stores in its water-resistant stock. Once stored properly, the weapon inside the stock will even float on water for a short while. The stock storage assembly includes two eight-round magazines.

Large caliber semiautomatic rifles are excellent choices for self-defense, great choices for large game and terrible choices for small game.

SELF-DEFENSE PURPOSES

Once again, I am not promoting reckless or unnecessary use of weapons against others. However, there may be times when self-defense is required. Following are three good choices for self-defense purposes:

AR15: This is the civilian derivative of the primary rifle utilized by the U.S. military. It utilizes a 5.56-millimeter round and most magazines hold 30 rounds of ammunition. It can easily be utilized for self-defense and used on large game. Due to its size, it is not a good choice for small game. There are dozens of manufacturers that offer these weapons and accessories to go with them.

AK-47: This is the weapon of choice for many countries throughout the world. It is a hearty weapon that does not need much maintenance to operative effectively. It utilizes a 7.62-millimeter round, which means it is effective for self-defense and large game as well. It is not a suggested round for small game.

BOLT-ACTION HUNTING RIFLES: There are so many in this category it would be difficult to pick out just one. Bolt-action rifles are single-shot weapons that reload by utilizing the manual bolt assembly. The engineering of these types of weapons are such that they are typically more accurate out to long distances than their semiautomatic counterparts. However, for the typical user, this is a negligible difference. For survival-related issues, you will not necessarily need to take shots out to that distance.

In summary, choose the rifle that fits the particular needs for what you foresee to be a possible issue. Rifles have "stand-off" capability, which means under an armed engagement, they will help you keep people at a much farther distance from you. Handguns, on the other hand, are much easier to carry and utilize in tight quarters without proper training. As I have attempted to make clear, please follow the appropriate laws of your area until such times that you live in a world that no longer has the rule of law in place.

BOWS

Bows are an incredibly useful device to bring down small and large game. They require an ample amount of practice to be able to do so. The benefit of utilizing one is that they are quiet and therefore do not bring attention to yourself. There are now bows that are specifically designed for the survival community as well. Bows come in two categories worthy of consideration: compound/longbow/recurve variants and crossbows. Each type warrants its own discussion.

Bows are great choices for large and small game, choose one designed to be taken down for ease in packing.

COMPOUND/LONGBOW/RECURVE VARIANTS

These are the typical bows that shoot arrows. Due to their nature, they will require much practice to be proficient in them. Bows should be judged on several different aspects:

- ➡ Effective bow length
- ➡ Storage length
- ➡ Corrosion resistance
- ➡ Durability
- ➡ Positive limb retention
- ➡ Protection of arrows
- ➡ Tools required for maintenance

With these thoughts in mind, you can easily see that a bow that is designed specifically for survival is a great choice. Most of the hunting-market bows are quite capable of doing the job effectively, but they lack the portability that a dedicated survival bow can offer. I chose the Survival Archery Systems Tactical Survival Bow to put in my go bag. It is the only bow currently available that keeps the breakdown arrows inside the riser. It is also incredibly corrosion resistant, which means I can put it in my go bag and not be concerned it will be corroded or otherwise ineffective when I get it out to utilize it.

In a survival situation, all bows of this type must be utilized with two strong arms for efficient and effective use. If you are injured in either arm, you will be unable to properly utilize them for this purpose.

CROSSBOWS

Crossbows are much more accurate and easier to use for beginners. They do take up a fair amount of space and do not break down easily. This means they are not easy to carry long-term or disassembled in a pack. They do require a fair amount of strength to load, but they give the user the ability to be utilized one-handed if he or she is injured.

PRIMITIVE TOOLS

There are many primitive tools that indigenous people used to defend themselves from animals and others. I have detailed several of them in Chapter 13. In this particular section, I want to consider them for self-defense tools. Many thanks to my good friends Doug Meyer and Johnny Faulkner for helping me learn how to utilize primitive skills and to develop tools of this nature. Following is a list of primitive tools that will enable you to defend yourself:

With the right technique and skill, and atlatl can be used to throw a dart long-distance.

ATLATL: The art of throwing a spear over long distances was a useful skill set for those who used them. Those who could throw the longest were those who had the longest arm. This is simply because of the physics involved of throwing one properly. Therefore, early peoples developed the atlatl as a way of effectively extending your arm. The components of an atlatl consist of a short stick and a long spear, also called a dart, with the stick held in the hand and connected to the spear. The spear can be fixed with a flint or similar spear point and is kept in proper trajectory by feather fletchings. The stick portion is near the length of the user's forearm and the spear can be much longer than the person themselves. This primitive tool had incredible reach. With proper technique, primitive humans could accurately throw these weapons well over 100 yards (91 m). Atlatls are the devices of their day with the longest stand-off capability.

BLOWGUNS: When made from cane and similar hollow plants, these weapons can be put together in a short amount of time. My teacher, Doug Myer, has an extensive background in the manufacture, use and history of these weapons. His research suggests that blowguns could easily be used and then discarded when no longer needed. Darts made from short sticks with feather or downy fletchings made these effective tools for game and self-defense. When used for self-defense, a blowgun would require great amounts of training for accuracy. This constraint can be counterbalanced by utilizing darts with toxins or bacteria on them to cause the intended prey to die of sickness.

With training, blowguns and atlatls can be made from the environment when no weapons are available.

RABBIT STICKS/AXES: These are handheld weapons that require the user to be in close proximity to the person or animal aggressing them. They should be utilized as a last resort because such a confrontation will most likely leave the user injured as well. Aggression and physical assault does not happen in the real world like it does in TV and movies. If you must engage in such activities, you are likely to be injured to some extent—even if you adequately defend yourself.

I hope I have made it clear that gear is an excellent way to extend yourself in uncomfortable situations. It extends your comfort level, which in turn extends your morale, which leads to a more productive and effective you. The key on all things related to gear is to get what works for you. This means that you should take my suggestions and practice them. I have had many successes (and failures) that put me in a good position to recommend these pieces. Once you start developing your kit, do not let it be new and shiny for long. Immediately get out and practice with your gear and take a class, workshop or other training. In this manner, you can get out and see what is working for you.

CHAPTER 17

A VISIT TO REALITY

AND THIS OUR LIFE EXEMPT FROM PUBLIC HAUNT, FINDS TONGUES IN TREES, BOOKS IN THE RUNNING BROOKS, SERMONS IN STONES AND GOOD IN EVERYTHING. . . . ONE TOUCH OF NATURE MAKES THE WHOLE WORLD KIN.

—WILLIAM SHAKESPEARE

It was a chilly but sunny day in the hills of Kentucky as a family of four ventured out to enjoy the glorious splendor that the dying leaves of scarlet red, golden yellow and dark, rich brown brought to the landscape.

The father, who was an experienced outdoorsman, was excited to take his mostly inexperienced-in-the-outdoors wife and their two small children out for their first overnight hike as a family. Each were excited in their own ways. The wife was happy to get away from the problems that arise from teaching and daily care of two kids. The kids were excited simply because they were kids and they had been born in a family with a healthy love of nature and being outside.

Upon reaching their initial destination, the family found a small creek that was normally passable, but was a bit higher than normal due to recent rains. The father, having previous knowledge of the area, knew another area that would meet their needs but verified its location with his map and compass. He had already left word with extended family that if his nuclear family could not stay in their intended location that they would go to one of two other locations. He marked those on a map and left it with the extended family members and told them to expect a call from him once they were out of the woods and safely home. He advised that it would be no later than 2 p.m. the next day.

The new location was only 1 mile (1.6 km) away on a well-marked and easily accessible trail. Halfway into the hike, it started to rain. The family each had their own ponchos, so they quickly got them out and put them on. This provided them with the necessary coverage to keep both themselves and the gear in their backpacks dry.

Shortly thereafter, they arrived at their destination, which was near a rock wall that provided good coverage from the winds and an excellent fire reflector for the rest of the evening. The father had been here many times and knew it would be a great place to get out of the wind and rain and set up camp.

Set up camp he did, with the help of little hands finding stakes and learning about knots. During that process, the mother gathered firewood from beneath another rock overhang (this provided an excellent coverage for the wood that was completely dry, even after the recent and current rain).

Beds were made out of dry leaves found in yet another rock overhang and brought to the campsite using tarps to carry them. This provided excellent insulating material against the cold ground. Sleeping bags were placed on top of the leaves. Everyone took time once camp was set up to drink water that was first boiled in their metal water bottles and then further purified by a water filter.

Once everyone was hydrated well, backpacker meals and other snacks were pulled out of various packs for dinner. The father fired up his white gas backpacker stove to boil more water for this endeavor. He first placed it on a stable rock to ensure nothing tipped over during the boiling process.

There were no bears in the area, so cooking food at their sleeping camp was not an issue. The father did carry with him a sidearm for the safety of his young family. Fortunately, there was no such need for it during this trip.

After dinner, everyone enjoyed some stories around the fire and then snuggled up in the sleeping bags and went off to sleep. The kids were placed between the parents in case they awoke in the night, confused regarding their location and needed some reassurance that all was okay. However, everyone slept well, with only the occasional unfamiliar sounds waking the parents.

The next morning, everyone packed up, buried any remnants of their fire lay and raked leaves about with branches in an attempt to bring it back to its natural state. When they were ready to leave, the father showed his kids how they had overturned leaves and broke a branch or two on their way in. They then backtracked that disturbance to the very short walk back to the trail they came in on. They hiked the 1 mile (1.6 km) back to the vehicle and left, refreshed from being outside.

This is the only story I have shared with you that has some half-truths in it. I say that because everything is true, but it's actually an amalgamation of stories from my own family's experiences. I did this to show you the ways that you can derive great enjoyment from spending time outdoors. There are a few things to note from this story in regard to safety and survival:

➡ My family could not go to our intended destination. This was quickly resolved with my experience and map-reading skills.

➡ The rain was unexpected. I had gear pieces to help ward off the rain and to keep our gear dry.

➡ Woods knowledge on how to find dry material for bedding and fire came into great use with the situations we found ourselves in.

➡ Safety measures were taken with the stove, placement of sleeping positions and camp itself to make it comfortable and such that the opportunity for injury was minimal (if not nonexistent).

➡ Before and after the trip, family members were notified of our intended locations *and* contingency locations. The family members were also given a time to notify authorities if we did not report back in a timely fashion.

➡ Tracking skills were used to go off the trail a bit and, most importantly, to find our way back to the trail.

So, after all these years of my outdoor experiences, why do I still enjoy being outside? Consider the following statistics:

➡ The average American child spends about half as much time outside than compared to children twenty years ago.

➡ Only six percent of children will play outside on their own in a typical week.

➡ On average, we spend eight hours per day watching television, playing video games or using a computer, tablet or phone for recreational purposes.

➡ Americans now spend 93 percent of their time inside a building or vehicle.

What does it matter? It is just a sign of the times, right? That is true, but consider the following:

➡ A study by the National Academy of Sciences showed that a 90-minute walk through a natural environment had a huge positive impact on participants.

➡ In that same study, researchers completed brain scans of the participants and discovered that physiologically, our brains are better equipped to handle stress after just 90 minutes of outdoor time.

➡ In a 2012 study, researchers discovered that after a four-day hiking trip in the wilderness, participants scored 50 percent higher on a creativity test. This allows you to be a much better problem solver.

- A 2004 study came to the conclusion that a good hike reduces the symptoms of ADHD, regardless of age, health or other characteristics that change with medication.

- A 2010 study in the *Journal of Environmental Science & Technology* showed that even a five-minute walk in the outdoors increases self-esteem. Spending the day outdoors had an exponential effect. It was also determined that walking near water had the biggest effect.

I think you get my point. We all need to be outside more. It will help you be calmer, more productive and more effective in all that you do. There are barriers to getting outside that are hard to overcome. One of these is access to suitable public or private land on which you can practice your skills. With a small bit of homework, you can find those locations. Go to an outdoor store. Ask the staff there, where to go. Contact federal, state and local fish and wildlife, natural resources or tourism departments and ask them where you need to go to get outside.

The second big barrier to getting outside is fear of the unknown in the outdoors. It is my strongest desire that I have taught you the way to getting outside more. In so doing, you are more prepared to safely enjoy nature. It is an even stronger desire of mine that you never run into any predicament in which you need to put survival skills and gear into play. Now that you have taken the effort to make it through this book, that should no longer be an issue. I have offered you the best I can in the way of mind-set, skills, tactics and gear to help you be ready for a survival situation.

It is now up to you to get outside and enjoy all that a natural wilderness has to offer.

As for me, I hope to see you on—or off—the trail!

SUGGESTED READING AND TRAINING FOR FURTHER INSTRUCTION

The following is a list of resources that I can very comfortably recommend. Many of these resources are the ones that have helped me to develop my own understanding of the various pieces of the survival puzzle that I call mind-set, skills, tactics and gear.

Also listed are the schools that I have either attended or otherwise have professional relationships with and feel comfortable recommending for further training and study. Online training is good if it is your only choice. The recommended schools I have listed here are those that I have trained with that offer hands-on learning. I believe it is *the* way for you to develop your skills. You can do it on your own by spending countless hours studying and practicing. However, you can attend a school and lean on the experience and understanding of teachers who have already spent the time practicing and honing their craft. The majority of these schools regularly teach classes throughout the United States. Please reference the websites listed to learn where and when classes are available.

Please note that I teach hands-on workshops and lengthy courses throughout the United States. I would be most pleased if you would choose Nature Reliance School as your choice for outdoor education.

MIND-SET

Alwood, Kelly. *Behavioral Programming: The Manipulation of Social Interaction*. CreateSpace Independent Publishing Platform, 2015.

Ayres, James. *The Tao of Survival: Skills to Keep You Alive*. Layton, UT: Gibbs Smith, 2013.

Gonzales, Laurence. *Deep Survival: Who Lives, Who Dies, and Why*. New York: W. W. Norton & Company, 2004.

Kabat-Zinn, Jon. *Wherever You Go, There You Are*. New York: Hachette Books, 2005.

Stroud, Les. *Will to Live: Dispatches from the Edge of Survival*. N. p.: Stroud Publishing, 2011.

SKILLS

Alton, Joseph and Amy Alton. *The Survival Medicine Handbook: A Guide for When Help Is Not on the Way*. N. p.: Doom and Bloom, 2014.

Beard, Daniel. *Camp-Lore and Woodcraft*. Mineola, NY: Dover, 2006. First published 1920 by Garden City Publishing Company.

Canterbury, Dave. *Bushcraft 101: A Field Guide to the Art of Wilderness Survival*. Avon, MA: Adams Media, 2014.

Coffee, Hugh. *Ditch Medicine: Advanced Field Procedures for Emergencies*. Boulder, CO: Paladin Press, 1993.

Hawke, Mykel. *Hawke's Green Beret Survival Manual: Essential Strategies For: Shelter and Water, Food and Fire, Tools and Medicine, Navigation and Signaling, Survival Psychology and Getting Out Alive!* Philadelphia, PA: Running Press, 2012.

Kochanski, Mors. *Bushcraft: Outdoor Skills and Wilderness Survival*. New ed. Auburn, WA: Lone Pine, 2016.

Lundin, Cody. *98.6 Degrees: The Art of Keeping Your Ass Alive*. Layton, UT: Gibbs Smith, 2003.

Olsen, Larry Dean. *Outdoor Survival Skills*. Provo, UT: Brigham Young University Press, 1967.

TACTICS

Hull, David Michael. *Man Tracking In Law Enforcement*. N. p.: VITALE, 2015.

Hurth, John. *Combat Tracking Guide*. Mechanicsburg, PA: Stackpole Books, 2012.

Scott-Donelan, David. *Tactical Tracking Operations: The Essential Guide for Military and Police Trackers*. Boulder, CO: Paladin Press, 1998.

Velocity, Max. *Contact! A Tactical Manual for Post Collapse Survival*. CreateSpace Independent Publishing Platform, 2012.

GEAR

Stewart, Creek. *Build the Perfect Bug Out Bag: Your 72-Hour Disaster Survival Kit*. Cincinnati: Betterway Home, 2012.

NATURE STUDY

Brill, Steve. *Identifying and Harvesting Edible and Medicinal Plants in Wild (and Not So Wild) Places*. New York: William Morrow Paperbacks, 2010.

Comstock, Anna. *Handbook of Nature Study*. Ithaca, NY: Comstock Publishing / Cornell University Press, 1986.

Peterson, Lee Allen. *A Field Guide to Edible Wild Plants: Eastern and Central North America*. The Peterson Field Guide Series 23. New York: Houghton Mifflin Harcourt, 1999.

SURVIVAL SCHOOLS

Nature Reliance School (my school offering primarily hands-on training, along with a very active blog and YouTube channel), www.naturereliance.org

Iron Sight Defense, ironsightdefense.com

The Scott-Donelan Tracking School, www.trackingoperations.com

TÝR Group, www.tyrgroupllc.com

Natural Awareness Tracking School, www.trackingschool.com

Earth School, www.lovetheearth.com

Midwest Native Skills Institute, www.survivalschool.com

Ultimate Survival Tips (online and hands-on training), www.ultimatesurvivaltips.com

ACKNOWLEDGMENTS

Will Kiester and Sarah Monroe at Page Street Publishing have been nothing short of incredibly professional, educational and helpful to me as a first-time book author. Will's vision and insight is incredible. Sarah's communication and editing has been utterly invaluable on so many levels. Her insight into this project was enlightening to say the least. Nichole Kraft of Paper Weight Editing was gracious and kind through the copyediting process. Page Street is top-notch!

My family has been supportive to an extent that overwhelms me at times. There is no bigger supporter of all that I do than my wife. Jennifer has remained steadfastly supportive of me when no one else was. I cannot imagine doing anything I have accomplished without her support. My kids, Lily and Zane (and now son-in-law Curtis), have brought me so much joy by joining me on outdoor trips so numerous that it is impossible to remember them all. From picnics and swims at "our spot" to hot chocolate in blinding snow and heavy rain, they have joined me in pursuing the outdoors as a means of challenging, nurturing and growing ourselves. My parents started this life of mine by allowing me to play outside nearly as much as I wanted, and taking me on more camping trips than amusement-park trips as I grew up. Where better to get amused and have fun than in the woods? My parents, and especially my in-laws, have been financially supportive to us in a way that has made my pursuits of teaching others possible. Teaching others is often not financially rewarding. Their support in this manner has been incredible.

To my brotherhood and larger Nature Reliance School community, I cannot thank you enough. I call Tracy Trimble my brother not because we are blood kin or because it sounds cool—Tracy has been a mentor, teacher and supporter to me as only a brother could. Even though he snores like a bear, I rather enjoy sharing a campfire with him. Kavin, Jacob and again my son, Zane, have been on so many trips, I also cannot remember them all. Their support behind the scenes at classes made it possible for me to do what I do in front of people. To the larger Nature Reliance School family of friends, students, followers, subscribers and more, I cannot thank you enough. Your encouragement has been the fuel that kept me going and will continue to propel all of us forward as a community of people who support, educate and encourage one another in outdoor pursuits.

My friend Brian Eury has told me to use his land as if it was my own and I could not thank him enough. It is his land that provided the early testing ground for Nature Reliance School classes. It was also in his cabin that 95 percent of this book was written. There is no electricity, running water or Wi-Fi there, which made it the perfect place to write a book on being outdoors. Many thanks to him for allowing me to take over his cabin for so many months.

My unofficial "pre-editing" team was great to help correct and educate me on various sections of the book. My wife read the whole book and offered insight, vision and assistance throughout. Others included Tracy Trimble on the land navigation and various other parts, Tali Hunt on the medical and first aid portions, Meido Moore on mindfulness and Rodney Vanzant on the tactical portions. Josh Carroll emailed and had several phone conversations with me that helped form this book in a very special way.

My teachers are numerous. My Creator, who made a world that is full of unanswerable questions and instilled a desire in me to try to find the answers anyway. Another nod to my dad, Frank, who taught me well enough that one day he surprised me and simply walked off in the woods so I could hunt squirrels on my own. I was very scared as a young boy as I watched him walk around the bend of the trail, leaving me alone. He taught me woods skills. More importantly, he taught me ethics that are used in the woods and in daily life. I have also sought out other instructors in an unending effort on my part to learn more: Rodney Vanzant of Iron Sight Defense, Mike Hull and Cornelius Nash of The Scott-Donelan Tracking School, John Hurth of TÝR Group and numerous biologists and foresters from the Kentucky Department of Fish and Wildlife and Kentucky Division of Forestry. I am incredibly fortunate to have trained with some of the best primitive technologists in the world, Doug Meyer and Johnny Faulkner, who are fine gentleman and gifted teachers. I have attended training led by peers in the same field of study that I teach—Richard Cleveland of Earth School and Tom Laskowski of Midwest Native Skills Institute are kind and gifted teachers. These teachers had a profound influence on the material found in this book.

On a professional level, I want to thank Matt Longley of Dan's Depot. He had vision of what I was capable of when I did not see it in myself. His marketing savvy helped guide me so that I could educate more people than I imagined I ever could. Scott "Bama" Moore is one of the finest men I know. He has been on the other end of the phone and behind the camera for me too many times to count. His encouragement and help has been greatly appreciated.

To you, the purchaser and reader of this book: I want to thank you. You are part of the Nature Reliance School family now. Don't put this book on a shelf. Take this book (or the knowledge from it) and practice your skills in a wilderness. Take this information and make it your own.

ABOUT THE AUTHOR

CRAIG CAUDILL began his outdoor experience while growing up hunting, fishing and playing in the woods of Kentucky. He has actively pursued experiential knowledge of all things related to wilderness recreation, living and survival. As a lover of history, he has studied and trained in primitive skills as well as modern methods to successfully challenge himself in the outdoors. He regularly teaches corporations, government agencies, universities and the public sector in these methods as a means of safety and team building. You can often find him teaching various law enforcement agencies and search and rescue teams in the science of man-tracking skills. He has been featured on the TV shows *Kentucky Afield*, *Kentucky Life* and *Tim Farmer's Country Kitchen*. He has also been interviewed on local news segments to share safety and survival skills. His written work has been featured in *Self-Reliance Illustrated*, *Wilderness Way*, *American Frontiersman* and *American Survival Guide* magazines. He has a very active blog and also guest blogs for Dan's Depot, Survival Life, Knowledge Weighs Nothing, How to Survive Stuff, Destiny Survival, Prepper Link, Survival Mom, Natural News, Family Protection Association and American Gun Association. He has an active YouTube channel, in which he provides free education on all things outdoors. His website can be found at www.naturereliance.org.

INDEX